A Little Book On

'MASTERY'

By

Julia Woodman

previously known as the poet, artist, and magazine editor

Jay Woodman

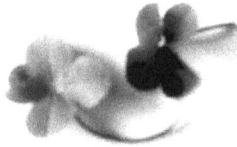

First edition 2016
© **Julia Woodman (both text & art)**
All rights reserved.

ISBN: 1-897920-84-9
Woodman's Press
46a Marlborough Hill, Dorking, Surrey, RH4 2DD

BOOKS WITH

H E A R T

INDEX

Information about Julia Woodman's other books
is on her website radiance-solutions.co.uk, plus on Amazon.

There are several other books of this nature,
plus quite a bit of poetry (as Jay Woodman).

Julia is also writing a novel,
which will probably be the first of several.

Namaste!

Intro: **Imperatives for a Masterful Life – Awareness and Intention**

We live in a reality which is built from the sum total of what we have been taught and what we have experienced so far. Everybody's reality is thus slightly different. It's as if we are having our own dreams of the world.

Dreams are pretty chaotic unless you learn to control them and dream lucidly. They're full of weird things, distorted events, illogical actions, and highly charged emotional responses. Hang on a minute, isn't life a bit like that?

You get upset about something your girlfriend said, and you storm off in the car and now you don't know what to say when you go back – if you go back. She doesn't know that you reacted that way because of something that happened in your past, so now she is angry because she thinks you are just being stupid, and in the process not considering how she feels.

Wouldn't it be better if we could just rewind that. Okay, so she says it and this time you still feel the twinge in your gut but you stop short to think for a sec – then you say "You know, yesterday that would have really upset me because of an incident in the past, but today I'm not going to let that trigger me into a silly reaction. Would you come sit next to me and let me explain? I'd like to share that story with you because it's still a part of me and I want to be open with you, after all, I love you so very much."

So this time, in that pause, you have become AWARE that you could have reacted immaturely to that trigger, and you have used your INTENTION to handle it differently. In fact you have turned the whole thing around into a positive situation. Now you are having an intimate discussion, opening up, trusting in your love. So instead of a nasty day you are having a good one. Well done you!

Now you can see how easily a bit of awareness and intention can be brought in to help. Surely you will see all sorts of other places you can use it in your life.

It can be a very useful thing to look at life as if we are in a matrix – a kind of net made out of opposites. You see, we must have some kind of construction to experience life in. If we did not have opposites, then how would we know what anything was – everything would just be the same. So we are in this space inside this net, stretched apart by the polar opposites, and we react to them as if they were really real. But if we looked at them as if they were just useful things to allow us to experience life, then we would actually experience life in a much more constructive way. With AWARENESS we can use this matrix to help us learn to live as we INTEND – consciously.

Oh we do live as we intend, but usually rather unconsciously, and because it is unconscious it tends to be very haphazard – whereas if we can do it consciously, we would be so much more in control – mastering ourselves.

So if we use this idea of a net as a tool to let us step back and see the big picture instead of being so caught up in it – we will see many ways of doing things differently.

My book – "No Paradox" – looks at all of this in detail, and examines different States of Consciousness too. Apart from that, there are many ideas and tips to help anyone get the best out of life.

My books, articles, websites, and social media pages all offer "Tools for our Conscious Journeying". Please feel free to share these widely.

Please also take a look at our new website in preparation for my book "Back to The Garden" – www.backtothegarden.org.uk and request membership of our open facebook group "Back to The Garden", as anyone can make input there.

Budhha said:
"By your own efforts waken yourself, watch yourself,
and live joyfully. You are the master."

Jesus said:
"These things and more shall you do after me."

So called 'MASTERY' and what it might be, or mean.

The soul is like a template to guide us, with frequencies of light and sound linked in to our physical bodies. The heart-centre is a more reliable base to work from than our brains, and we can in fact master our minds and train them to always work for us instead of against us as they sometimes do. We know in our heart of hearts, the core of our beings, who we really are, and how we should live. It's just that we get caught up in our busy minds with a bunch of external / internal stuff, which distracts us from this, until we forget it's even there.

I think it's fine that we have used our minds for so many things, but focusing on that area so much has also been very destructive, and we have allowed ourselves to be led astray by others who wish to control us and plunder the planet.

It is time to return to the heart - to use our minds in more heart-centred ways to create better modes of living, personally and globally. We can then use our minds to create what we truly need, instead of making all these false starts, and sabotaging ourselves.

We should also be very aware of what we put into & on our bodies, as they are our homes here – we need to avoid toxins, keep hydrated, breathe, sleep, and exercise properly, and generally take care of ourselves. This will help maximise the quality of our life experience.

So 'Mastery' means not filling our minds and bodies with junk, plus learning to get to grips with our true selves in such a way that we live consistently in balance with ourselves and the world around us, not over-reacting to anything. We learn to keep everything in perspective – a perspective we choose to believe works best for us, and thus wish to reflect in our lives here. However, that perspective tends to constantly get updated as we experience and learn more. Although I don't really think that we ever stop learning, I think we might eventually get to a place where we are pretty consistent in what that perspective is. And thus mastery of self is living in accordance with that.

Don't be too hard on yourself though if you slip up sometimes – we all do that, no matter how hard we try. The thing is to listen to valid criticism, note other's responses, and be aware of mistakes so that we can learn from them. This does not mean trying to please everybody - you are simply checking that you are keeping to your consciously chosen path / way of being; taking new information into account, and fine-tuning details if warranted.

Roundup - Beliefs & Aims

I believe that we are here to evolve – to learn by experience – and continue to evolve physically, mentally, emotionally, spiritually, consciously (once we are able to) through the lives we create – (conscious evolution) through one life after another until eventually we return to the source of all life (whatever we may conceive that to be) – 'perfect'. Except by then you would no longer be aware of what 'perfection' was, as you would just be part of that stream again.

And that in the first place is perhaps why we are sent out - to gather experience, and feed back a constant flow, so that the stream has something to perceive outside of itself, and thus it can feel as if it is alive instead of just holding the potential of life. So we must be connected to it in order for it to experience our journeys with us.

And perhaps the stream desires a greater and greater flow and that is why we multiply and divide the energy even further out, creating more things to experience and more souls to experience them. Or perhaps the stream cannot be conscious enough to decide, being just pure energy, and it all just happens, creation and destruction and more creation, over and over again, automatically. Either way, the conscious universe itself surely expands / evolves.

Cycles are witnessed everywhere in nature, birth, death, and rebirth, even amongst the planets themselves. Patterns are repeated in cells of plants and in journeys of stars. We look out, thinking that we are somehow special, the most conscious of creations, able to imagine, able to create ourselves, able to witness and learn, able to analyse what we are and what our lives might be about, able to fully weigh things up and make choices; but do we really earn or deserve that 'specialness'? Are we conscious enough, or are we just one more life-form in a stream of life forms coming & going? Do we take enough care of ourselves and our home-planet? Do we treat animals and plants with enough kindness & respect? Do we even extend enough kindness and respect to our own fellows?

If you are alive then you still have something to learn from this lifetime, though that may perhaps be for nothing more than the perception of experience along the way. So – at the same time as striving towards 'perfection', I can also understand nihilism! Everything vanishes. If we are ONE with the Stream, God, or Universe, then we are everything and yet nothing. Everything vanishes! Nada. But it starts again...... We come from nothingness and return to nothingness - yet the cycle is infinite. Poets strive to understand this, artists, scientists, anyone who is driven to try to gain some understanding of the universe, and / or our minds and natures.

I should explain here that by 'perfection' I do not mean some ultimate amazingly perfect state of 'mastery', I actually just mean being perfectly human, which is to make mistakes but to be aware enough to learn from them, and to try to be the best one can be, given what one is aware of at each stage of your journey.

I would like to quote a bit of Andrew Cohen for you here:

At the Heart of the Paradox

"The ultimate spiritual revelation is that there is no other. There is only One When any individual goes very deep into a meditative state, momentarily transcending the separate self-sense or narcissistic ego, this profound singularity at the level of consciousness itself is what he or she will find. There is an uncontainable thrill in those moments when the non-relative nature of consciousness actually becomes apparent… Matter, mind, and time are all relative. Consciousness is not."

And here's new a bit from me:

In the Essential Core of us
I believe there is something Pure.
We can feel it in stillness
where only our heartbeats and breathing
remind us we exist at all.

We can draw on it to renew us, inspire us,
support us, guide us forwards,
help us decide how we want to live.
It opens us to more, and more, consciousness,
it gives us, and give us - life itself.

*

"There is an imperative to be in a process - the given energy & consciousness of life means for us to be constantly observing, learning, becoming - and extending that process of creation/evolution."
Joules

8

What is the Source of Life?

God is just one of many names we give to that which we perceive as an all encompassing power / energy / love / consciousness… or source of all life – the same thing that quantum physicists call the quantum field – that which holds the possibility of all things, that which can become matter and return to energy, and seems to have some sort of imperative to do so, that which is inside of us as well as all around us.

But religion limits this, personifying the various Gods as egoic, wrathful entities trying to command and control us, tying religions up into packages each group protects and defends, causing dissent in our world where there should be unity and compassion.

I once had some irreverent fun thinking up things that the letters G.O.D. could be an acronym for, and think that "Ground Of Dimensions" was the best, but of course the word doesn't come from English…. reading about it's many possible origins is a fascinating and surprising exercise actually. There seem to be roots of it in many different places, including Germanic Gothic tribes, for example. In earlier research I saw that different religions seem to mostly stem from Abraham's sons anyway – all one family! So how did it get so separated out that men fight over it?

I can't believe that {any God} would require us to do anything. Why would a supposedly all powerful perfect {Being} have any need for us to do anything except be ourselves? Eventually we (the soulful deeply conscious strand of us) must come back to the source, no matter how long it takes, and (by the way) no matter what that source actually is. Why should {a God} be wrathful and punish (or reward) us? If {He} were a person, then I can imagine that (as for a parent), it would be hard to always be patient, and not get frustrated with the silliness of {His} children, making the same mistakes over and over again, but if he were this supposedly perfect {Being} then {He} wouldn't get angry anyway, and {He} would also know that it does not ultimately matter. If {He} were indeed a {Being} then surely he would just chuckle fondly. Or, if 'God' is not a person, but an energy field, then this field would not command us anyway. Things, including us, would simply arise, go forth, and eventually return.

I do think that Jesus was a real person, learning to be a master, as many others have done and are doing. I think he had to let things happen – let the fear of those people run its course, and learn to trust that his love and the love of what he believed in was so complete that it would overcome all. Even he doubted sometimes. As for miracles, he also said that we would do what he could do, and more.

I tend to always return to thinking that the nature of any 'God' should be more like the things I mentioned in the first paragraph.

I believe that this field, or life force, is everywhere around us as well as within us, permeating our every cell. (May the Force be with you! Minus the armoured spaceships please.) I believe that it is when we are in a peaceful state of alignment with it, that we most affect things around us, just by consciously being that, not by rushing around trying to change things with great effort, as Ken Wilber discusses.

I do think we need to make changes though, just that we should do this in very conscious & organic ways – a natural RE-LOVE-UTION and an EVOLUTION towards becoming a more CONSCIOUSLY balanced, loving, sustainable species. Perhaps to become more 'God' like, if you wish to put it that way, but to reiterate, I mean in the sense of being GRACE filled, and willing to be part of a team for betterment of all people, animals, plants, and the planet.

Ken Wilber's books actually gave me great hope because he talks about things that are already being done in politics and economics, areas where I thought we were pretty thin on using higher levels of consciousness.

Yet on the other hand it is scary, in that he points out that groups at only basic levels of consciousness now have access to stuff that has been created by those at higher levels, so the information is unlikely to always be used with appropriate responsibility.

Once I might have suggested that we could only access certain knowledge levels when we had developed enough maturity to be responsible for handling it appropriately, but that's really not the case. Gosh, that would have been such a useful fail-safe to prevent humanity from getting into so much trouble with our own inventiveness!

Greed and ego seem to be even more of a problem, with some going to all ends to gain control of everyone & everything. Where would it actually get them though, to have piles of wealth and a few unhealthy surviving slaves in a burned out world? It seems stupidity isn't a fail-safe either. But then, perhaps I judge too harshly, when I should follow my own advice and judge not at all.

We do have to see where there are things that need to be brought back into balance though, if we are going to sort out humanity's team, and evolve into better beings collectively. It feels like the source of life, whatever it is exactly, does care that we do this. I'm not sure how it appears to have feeling, but as it is within each of us as our life force, I guess that just makes sense because we know we love life and don't want to give up on it, so it's reflecting our emotion really. Or perhaps it is a simple and logical imperative – life preserves life.

It seems, with humanity, that power is the crux here - whether it's an ego-driven power or a grace-filled power. Inventiveness that gets out of hand (so that it becomes destructive), selfishness, and greed - all seem to stem from ego-driven power. So here's a thought - perhaps that is what went wrong with GOD…. When they threw out the Gnostics and rewrote the Bible, the whole concept of God became ego-based. Rulers used religion as a tool to command over us, and it became a heresy to believe that God lived within us as a pure creative and sustaining life force. In the hands of ego-driven power, one of the halo's – O – fell off the original word – GOOD, and it became this three-quarter pretence of itself. Thought I'd have a bit of a laugh with all that, sorry about my urge to play with words, but hey, everyone is playing games with us all the time it seems. Of course, I've used English / Christianity here, but other religions often have similar patterns. I don't understand why anyone would surrender their innate power to a 'leader' promoting difference & violence. It's just a huge misrepresentation via ego-based men though, nothing to do with truly spiritual religious experience. At the deep spiritual level we are all one. No division exists between groups of any sort.

The grasping, posturing, ego is like a little devil we have to subdue in our journeys towards enlightened consciousness - whatever route we choose to take. The ego has a useful function, but we need to master it, instead of allowing it to overbear our hearts & souls. We ought to be using the pure sense of power, stemming from goodness & right consciousness, to help get things back into some sort of balance. Aligning ourselves with the original pure source of life, ensures we keep ourselves pure – while we get on with both the practical & spiritual things that need to be done here. Yes, the little work of men does matter - it has to be our responsibility to clean up our act & settle some things on our home planet. If we sit back and do nothing, it's pretty obvious what will happen.

Does what we Believe affect what Happens to us?

Damn sure it does! I believe that our thoughts can create our reality – what we see is created by our thoughts and expectations. If you grow up having been told to watch out for certain things then you kind of expect those things to crop up. If you focus on negative expectations then you tend to get negative results. But if you set these aside, detach from them, then you may observe things differently. If you expect things to go right, then your very attitude helps to make that happen. This is not just with interactions with people by the way, it happens even with things you can't logically explain how you could have any influence over, but I trust it and am grateful that it works.

I think it is great if you can, to make a little time in the mornings before rushing off to work for example to do some stretching type exercises and maybe even sing a song like "Oh what a beautiful morning, oh what a beautiful day, oh what a wonderful feeling, everything's going my way." None of this needs to take a huge amount of time or preparation, in fact you can even sing as you walk, or in the car on the way if you prefer, and even just a couple of stretches makes a difference, the point is that you are giving your mind and body something positive to start the day with, just as important as breakfast really! We can also remind ourselves of things to be grateful for anytime – it's a good thing to do before falling asleep at night. Gratefulness really helps to focus on the positives, so does mindful noticing of small beautiful details in 'ordinary' moments of our lives.

Also, different people see things differently. One person might see a redundancy as a terrible blow (a forced end to something he believes he still needs to keep hold of), whereas another might see it as a nudge to get her started in a new direction. You can also help yourself deal with something by moving towards the second view, suddenly or gradually coming to the realisation that actually it does set you free, and you have more time to seek out things you are really interested in (instead of being stuck in a rut), and the whole thing turns into an exciting challenge, or opportunity, rather than a fearful event.

Our emotions and beliefs affect our physical well-being… we literally give ourselves hormonal and bio-chemical highs and lows according to what we are thinking (even if just reacting blindly), as shown in the movie "What the Bleep do we Know". Biologists are starting to pick up on this. All those missing pieces start to fall into place, and other bits can be explained now when they remember to bring consciousness into the story as both an inside and outside influence on our physical development.

If a person worries too much, or frets about wanting to escape something yet never faces up to the fact enough to do anything about this, they can literally cause themselves to become ill. If they hate a part of their body, that part might manifest problems. It is far better to learn to love and accept all parts of yourself and your path through life, accepting that you can learn to change along the way as your ideas of who you want to be and where you are going will inevitably change, via your discoveries, and as your awareness grows. (I had the idea of a computer game along these lines for young people.)

Cancer for example can often be cured by helping someone to change their attitudes, as well as using positive visualisations connected with loving themselves or a particularly affected part of their body, and envisaging the cancer clearing from their tissues; or indeed to support them in finding the strength to make important changes in their lives so that they will be more happy.

If you believe your mind and body to be sacred parts of you that are needed to live fully, along with your spirit or fundamental root of yourself, then they should be treated that way. If you don't believe that, then maybe a prayer that you will one day would go down well, along with any prayers you might make for the well-being of others and situations out in the world. Prayers are positive thoughts after all, reinforced by actual expression. It doesn't matter whether you believe in some God or not for them to work.

As a nutritional therapist I know just how important optimum nutrition is, and things like avoiding, or at least counteracting, toxic stuff, breathing and sleeping properly, and getting exercise. Good food and minimum stress can literally activate good parts of your DNA and switch off negative potentials.

Healers get intuitive help with healing. They often see incredible things, including the rainbow colours of different energy levels in the body and auras. These are clues to help us work with the energies, more than just our feelings, and sometimes we get messages too about particular things. All this can be pretty mind blowing, but we accept it, as the meaning and results all hang together so well, and other healers, and our patients, are often able to corroborate our experiences.

Sound healing is also very effective. Different colours and sounds have vibrations that can be channelled into the body and connected with the endocrine system to help relevant areas or organs, or into joints or muscles for example. Pythagoras is mostly known for his geometry, but he also used mathematics combined with harmonics in his sound healing school! The voice can create complete overtones - octaves behind each note, and the note will intuitively be of a particular shape (sort of vowels mostly), and you can literally feel your cells dancing with delight and aligning with the harmony of it. By the way, apparently a cat's purr is good for our bones.

I believe that generally, if we think positively then things are fine, and if we think negatively then things tend not to go so well. I believe that our expectations have a definite effect on what happens. If we walk under a cloud then we are literally creating that cloud – we could lift it at any time by developing a more sunny outlook. This does not mean we get irrationally silly, it means a quite simple change of focus to appreciate the good things rather than always moaning about the not so good, being grateful for what we do have (for example, a husband we can trust, growing children, our good health, food and shelter), rather than always yearning for something else.

Of course, all this gets a bit tricky for someone living in a war zone or natural disaster area, yet it is surprising how living in tough situations quite often seems to almost 'force' the human spirit to shine through! The rest of us could always do with being thankful for how well-off we are in comparison, and be ready to help where we can. Adverse conditions often bring people together too. Regardless of personal beliefs, people who might not normally mix will tend to team up to win through overall.

Going back to beliefs in general - we should limit our personal beliefs to our own lives, as we do not have a right to try to tell others what to believe. The best thing you can do is be an example of what you believe, just by being yourself. Be the change you wish to see in the world – as Ghandiji said. Change comes from within, not from outside. So it is okay to gently guide people who ask for guidance and let them take what they want from it and leave the rest, but it is surely not okay to try to force ideas upon people. They have to want to seek change themselves, and find their own answers from whatever information or experiences they then have access to. People are all journeying at their own levels, wherever they need to be at that time. I don't believe we should ever make judgements, although I know only too well how terribly easy it is to slip into doing this. People who have asked for guidance will learn from whatever they take within (they literally find their own answers from the absorbed information), but people you try to force things on will just reject the intrusion anyway. It is pure impertinence to try to interfere with their paths, and it also implies that we are judging them as 'wrong' in the first place!

In all the things one might try to do in life, I think that intention is all important. If you simply come from the heart and try to do your best in any situation, then you tend to manage to do so. Too much of anything else tends to only muddy the waters.

Healers focus on having the best intention for the patient, whatever is right for them, rather than harbouring their own ideas of what might be best for them. Some people may need to hold on to situations until they learn a particular lesson from them. Others may need to let go of life this time round for reasons of their own, perhaps coming back to learn more later, in a different set of circumstances. Bizarrely sometimes exactly the same type of circumstances could occur, though other factors - such as prior experiences, or attitude - would then turn out to be the variable, hopefully enabling them to get it at last. Have you noticed that life does this to you all the time anyway, even within one lifetime – if you don't get the message first time, then it will chuck you into more situations to try to show you that same message again and again until you click, especially if it's something you profess to know, but actually don't! It's a bit like reading a book or watching a movie you read or watched before, only this time you suddenly realise something different about it.

Counsellors help people find their own answers too, rather than trying to tell them what to do. Life Coaches mostly provide tools, and support of course, to help reach whatever goals you might choose for yourself. Even Stress Consultants show you rather than tell you, how to develop ways of easing a stressful overload.

So, it really is up to you to become increasingly aware. It's obviously great to ask for all the advice and help you could want, and to study widely - but ultimately it's your life to choose what to do with, and to grow into, through direct experience. Serious stuff, but hey, I'm sure we're meant to have fun with it too! Focus, awareness, intention, spirituality, even responsibility, and life itself – none of it's meant to be heavy. All of it can be light and joyful - that's when things work best.

What Really Matters?

Basically, I don't really think it matters too much what we believe, as long as we don't force it on other people or judge them for being different from us. For ourselves though, the main aim is to find a way to be happy, I'd say. Some people are lucky enough to be able to just say "I don't know what life is about so I might as well just enjoy it". Most of us also have some imperative to want to do what we believe to be 'good' stuff, and a conscience that somehow nags us if we don't. So we tend to find ways of being happy that also involve us doing at least some of this 'good' stuff. Generally it is not quite so easy for us just to detach enough to say "it doesn't matter what life means or where we come from or what will happen when we die" and be happy with that, not needing to have answers. Generally we try to build some sort of construct or framework of belief to live by. Whatever we believe to be true, we then tend to find things that fit in with that, thus sort of 'proving' our theories to ourselves, yet so many of us have different theories that may sound equally good to an objective ear! Even scientists do this at times.

The theory I have presented in my book "NO PARADOX" - is meant as a helpful idea, enabling us to step outside of the web of apparent opposites and take a more objective view of things at least some of the time. We should then be less reactively pulled about emotionally, and live with more equilibrium. This is necessary for us to be able to face up to some of the issues at large in the world, such as those I will discuss in my book "Back to The Garden", and on the www.backtothegarden.org.uk website. We also use global meditation link-ups to help keep us focused, and plant positive thought seeds into the collective consciousness to help evolve everything.

So, while at the same time as trying to show you that I think the constructs of paradoxes (amongst other things) are just that – constructs and not really real – I am also attempting to show you ways of detaching, letting go a bit, so that you can be truly happy. A construct can be useful of course, but it is better not to be too dependent on it, or attached to it, and to realise that it is actually just a framework to allow certain things to happen.

We can literally trick ourselves mentally into doing things differently through using meditation or even hypnosis or other tools, or we can achieve it by learning positive patterns of behaviour, or we can follow ideas and do exercises to help lead us to new understandings, and we can gradually change our philosophy.

My idea is just one way, to be sure, but I hope it will give you lots of tools and make you think, at the very least. Take from it what you want, and leave the rest, I don't expect everyone to go along with ALL of it, but I think that even bits of it might be quite useful.

Meditation is one of the most important tools for helping with mind, body, spirit balance. It improves overall health and helps your conscious development. It also really helps with things like studying, achieving optimum performance say in sports, and many other things.

There are actually many different kinds of meditation, and many ways of achieving the peak, but relaxed, mental state involved. Some meditations require nothing at all except to sit and watch an object such as a candle. Others require you to focus on breathing. Or you can use mantras and toning. Or you could take a meditative walk, or dance. Or you can use guided meditations to lead you into certain imaginary situations, or to help you deal with stress or certain issues.

I have many guided meditations available on YouTube and on my website, and I can write these according to people's needs. I even create them on the spot in group workshops to include things that those present have asked for.

...until the rushing world dissolves / into that one pool.
End of poem "Crossover" in "Following Father" with art from "Terra Affirmative".

What else might matter?

I think that drinking too much on a regular basis and depending on drugs etc are not ways of being happy, but ways of trying to shut off and make ourselves forget that we aren't happy yet, ways of being less conscious. So if we wake up, then we might be more likely to find answers than if we give up.

However, I don't think there is much wrong with drinking or using drugs sometimes, as an experience, or experiment, or a way of dealing with a state of mind – as long as one comes through the other side – and it is certainly possible to come out happier. It is possible to relax and use one's mind to imagine crawling through dark tunnels to explore your shadow side, or to imagine flitting through nature's beauty, or to examine a series of philosophical thoughts. One can often write or paint from such journeys, although my mind seems to do it without any such aids. The main thing I think is that you don't want to let things get a grip on you and drag you into negative spirals, or dependency, you need to maintain your own sense of power over who you are choosing to be. Dependency definitely numbs your consciousness, plus you tend to lose respect for yourself.

It is always down to individual choice though, and if that is what someone wants to do, then we should try to respect that choice I guess, while at the same time not entirely giving up on a friend who may someday ask for help to come back.

As I touched on before, taking care of all aspects of yourself is important, especially if you wish to optimise your life experience. Good diet, exercise, breathing well, sleeping well, avoiding or counteracting toxins in household products and toiletries, as well as in processed foods, and in many other things – are all significant - so is good communication, to minimize stress in all relationships, including at work..

I have nutritional therapy packages available by email, which include personalised initial assessments & ongoing support sessions.

Light up your Life

What can we learn to be?

I believe that I have been discarding many illusions one by one, especially since I started learning to be a healer, and reading all sorts of interesting personal development and philosophical books. First I began to believe that I had plenty of love, and then I found that indeed I did. However, it does keep on being tested, so that I can learn to be so in ANY circumstances. Both forgiveness and fear become irrelevant words if you can love unconditionally. This does not mean that I welcome any old person into my home, I still get to choose who my friends are! (While still dealing with forgiveness, it is always important to forgive yourself for any situation as well as the other person or people. This does not only apply to things you may have done, but to things you may not have done. It also applies to simply having allowed yourself to be sucked into that situation in the first place instead of moving gently beyond it.) It took me a long time to learn to love humankind in general as when I was very young I used to keep myself to myself, and mostly just loved nature, while despising some of the things that humans did. I guess I also felt safer with nature than with people to start with.

I mostly believed that I was happy despite whatever happened around me, and I found that I generally was. This also gets tested. Then gradually I began to believe in abundance, that I have everything I need to survive – to pay my way. This was a hard one for me! (I had to get rid of beliefs instilled in childhood that there was never enough, and that a woman did not have the right to have and do all that she wanted anyway, and replace those discarded beliefs with new ones.) There is no lack, everything I need already exists. I certainly have the right to want to have a family and a career and study and teach. I can do anything I dream of doing. We can learn to be anything we want to be. I do have to keep reminding myself of where I am up to though, as it is so easy to get distracted by the world out there and go off track a bit. It's amazing how my finances don't seem to add up at all if you look at the figures on paper, but here I am managing just fine from day to day, month to month, and through the years. I still have a way to go on this though, as I believe I should earn everything from doing what I feel I really should be doing, from using my strongest talents entirely, but at the time of writing I am still compromising a little more than I am comfortable with on that. I do enjoy doing all sorts of different jobs and using different skills though, and enjoy teamwork, plus keeping on the move a fair bit to keep the old bod from locking up too much (as it tends to do if just sitting writing, or on the computer). I gave up a full time job a few years ago, and moved to being part time (actually with a zero hours contract now, although I usually get offered more hours than I want, so I do have to say NO quite a lot), as well as being self-employed. My plan was to leave time to get my books written, showing that I mean to be following what seems to me to be my obvious path, and trust the process. It's working quite well, and although that common phrase "it could be better" springs to mind, I am actually very grateful for how things are going, and there is certainly great potential for it to keep improving.

Friendships and relationships came along to help me with many things especially trying to learn to communicate successfully, but communication seems to be one of the hardest things for human beings to get right. If you spend a lot of time with someone it seems that you are bound to get things wrong somewhere along the line, and you have to just hope that you both care enough to keep working it all out. Some spoke hardly at all, and others spoke a lot, so there was seldom a good balance. At first none of us knew how we should do things, then later on at least some of us did know, yet often still forgot, and I have to say that this is still an area I am working on.

Communication is very difficult if there is an imbalance between the participants. If one feels less able to face up to their emotions and speak out about things, then the other will be left guessing as to what they think and need. If one is afraid of the other's response, whether for real or imagined reasons, then it really does hamper things, and the one who is suppressing his emotions will become slowly outraged with pent up frustrations and resentments. If one makes themselves into a martyr, trying to be reliable and responsible at the expense of his own happiness, then it hurts the other one as well because she did not want that, there was really no need, they should have worked together as a team. In the end sometimes it seems better to walk away if you think you are causing someone to suffer and you can't seem to reach them to sort it out. Either way, it makes you feel terrible, although really you know it's not your fault; and don't expect them to thank you for setting them free! They may even curse you and blame you entirely, but you have to let it go. I am sorry I did not understand then more of what I know now because *maybe* that might have made enough difference, maybe not, but either way we have to learn to move on.

These days I seem to need to be quite assertive in my communication, both at home and in my job. I don't think it's a bad thing, but I find it unnatural for me if it entails actually having to butt in and speak up quite loudly. Sometimes I think I might actually overdo it, especially if other people are around with whom it isn't necessary - yet I tend to do it anyway as it is becoming a bit of a habit! So, as I am aware of this, I try to work on adjusting the balance. At other times I am still very quiet, especially if we are in a noisy environment where my soft tone cannot really be heard anyway, and quite often just because I don't really feel a need to contribute to the conversation. Generally I prefer to be quieter in the hope that other people will consider me and let me say my bit if the subject is something that affects me, but if they don't, then I know it would be unhealthy in the long run for me to always just go along with things, so I do make a point of butting in. There is a big difference between being assertive and being aggressive though, and sometimes people seem to forget that. To speak your truth gently is most effective (as long as people have enough respect to listen – so it's good to plan a special time to talk about important things).

I am open to trying different things, and hope to keep being conscious of what I say and think and do, as I am well aware that there is lots of room for error and misunderstanding.

It is good to try to focus on the positive, or at the very least to keep a balance. We need to be grateful when someone does do something, not just moan when they don't for instance, and try to be clear and direct rather than loading statements with emotion or threat. It has to go both ways, everyone has an equal right to be respected, listened to, considered, thanked, appreciated, etc, and we all have a right to stand up for our needs or to express our feelings and opinions.

Although we often operate as teams, or couples, we still each need to be true to who we are as individuals, so one certainly can't try to *make* someone else go along with something that doesn't sit well with them, or try to change them. Obviously people need to be given some freedom and trust to go out and do the things in life that are important to them, again as long as it works both ways, and one doesn't take the other for granted. All parties should contribute to the smooth running of a home or business, whether it be financial or tasks, one should not take advantage of the others all the time, as they will not put up with such unfairness for too long. We should teach our children these things by explaining why they need to start contributing, not just ordering them to start pulling their weight. We should teach them about bills etc too, so that they can one day manage properly on their own. It is not actually kind to just do everything for our kids, as how will they learn what they need to learn if you do?

Don't allow others to box you into a role either. If you want people to know who you are, then show yourself to be that person by doing things you really want to do with your life, and don't just get lumbered with housework all the time. Often we make too big a deal out of small things that don't really matter, and we all do stuff that kind of balances out the stuff that the other one does, so we should just accept that these kind of imperfections happen, and get on with it. However, we do need to communicate effectively to reach a fair understanding about issues that are important to us. If we can't find a balance that suits all parties, even with reasonable compromise, there is no use trying to hold on to an impossible situation. Honest and open discussions are key, we need to try to understand other people's points of view, and often learn some unexpected lessons!

We should not berate ourselves for not being able to perfectly manage in every situation. If we find ourselves in a situation not of our choosing, then it helps to remind ourselves why we are actually there and what our priorities are, so we take a step back from the rest of it and watch ourselves as we try different approaches to manage and learn from the situation. Sense of humour often helps, and can come to the fore if we are less drawn in. Sometimes things are due to simple misunderstandings for example due to different cultures and languages, sometimes people are just being pig-headed or bloody-minded.

We have to ultimately accept that we can't always agree on everything, and that is also okay.

There are many things in life we should walk away from, particularly bitter arguments and violence.

I believe that most of the human race is stuck in their throat chakras as we so often cannot seem to communicate without fighting. We should be able to rise above (or evolve beyond) this and be able to discuss / debate issues or differences of opinion without things getting out of hand, but there are so many reasons why we don't. Human beings generally struggle to say what we really need to say with clarity, and are not very good at listening properly (with unselfish respect) either. We are often afraid, because we allow emotions to get in the way, and worry about irrational reactions and loss of control over perceived needs, when really we could put that all aside, and truly talk!

There IS a lot of material available to help us master the skills of good communication, and it is surely a major part of our evolution to do so.

Oh by the way, one should always be able to laugh at one's self, whether for not realising things sooner, or just as a way of letting go of past tensions. One can also learn to laugh off comments that might have been hurtful before, because once you know yourself and approve of your journey, then it does not matter what other people think of you or of what you are doing.

I am only just beginning to realise that there is something else that I have plenty of – and that is time. Partly because we keep on coming round, and partly because we can manipulate it. This message has been given to me in so many ways… through other beings, through reading, through thinking, but it is always a challenge to remember and apply when continually re-adjusting to new patterns of work and living and sleeping. My wish is always to do more with EASE but it isn't that easy to actually achieve, especially if I get in my own way with unnecessary detail. I believe that I can do it all, and it is part of my reality to view it that way, simply because I choose to. I just have to keep practicing.

Internal communication, or self-talk, matters a lot. We tend to believe what we tell ourselves more than what other people tell us, so our subconscious begins to act accordingly. We can actually use meditation to calm our minds so that they stop getting in the way with incessant chatter and worry, and we can train them to work with us a lot more instead. Using affirmations for example, can build our self-esteem, and help us achieve things.

Once we are sufficiently aware, we can learn to evolve ourselves in whatever direction we want.

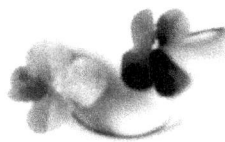

"There are always exquisite things and times
to remind us of the original source of all beauty and love."
Joules
"Being here to witness the beauty, to learn, to be astonished, to love, is enough.
Being able to create in addition is a delightful honour."
Joules

What does a 'master' know?

Please note that I do not really find the term 'master' very tasteful as I believe that we are all equal in that we are each at the right place we need to be at in our process of evolution, however I am not sure what other term to use for someone who has mastered certain concepts, or to use 'mastery' for something one might aim for.

I do not think that someone who has shut themselves away from 'normal' life is a 'master' as they probably cannot interact properly with 'normal' life if they need to be shut away from it. I think we need to learn to be able to exist at all levels to the best of our ability, and without being a 'pain' to others, but I also think that anybody is still bound to make mistakes sometimes. I just think that we should develop our own ways to live and try to follow those as much as we can. In that way at least we are being aware of what we are doing.

Some of the concepts of 'mastery' however, can be very useful ideas to go by, and they help us to move outside of the matrix of polarities. **It is not really that we learn to master our emotions, it is that we learn stuff that helps us to see things differently, therefore the emotions don't have their old grip, so can't tie us in knots any more.** We learn that some things are just not useful to us, or no longer relevant, and that other things are much more useful. **We become in fact masters of our bodies and minds, using them as tools to get us where we want to be, rather than being at their mercy.** Perhaps that is a better definition of what a 'master' is.

If you are willing to accept that we might have come to this planet as spiritual beings to learn what it is like to live life in the physical, then it is immediately obvious that the spirit is the master in truth. Even if you don't accept this, you kind of become aware of it once you start trying it out that way round. The body has its obvious limitations, the mind has its limitations too, only the spirit has the deep knowledge and the power to integrate everything and guide you towards living in the flow, learning, and experiencing life fully, being the person you have come here to be. A 'master' knows that it is better to be gentle, than to allow the ego to toss things around.

A 'master' knows that he/she is happy, and inherently safe, thus they are.

I am calm and loving instead of reacting and becoming impatient and angry because I know that I have all the time I want. Whatever happens just happens and there is always time. I do not take things personally. If my kids go to live with their Dad then it does not mean they do not love me. It means only that this is what they are doing at this time – it is easier for them now. I am happy in this moment to allow the universe to proceed - in fact I am glad he gets a chance to spend time with them. They know I love them no matter what any of us do. I am active, and yet still. I do things, but hold a peace within, a connection with my inner thread of being, a connection with the earth, and with the universe out there too.

I believe that we can access this all-encompassing powerful energy field to find out anything we wish to know or achieve anything we wish to achieve. We only need to know how to tune into it, how to fine-tune ourselves to be receptive instruments, and how to ask the right questions. (For example, in water-divining etc you need to be very specific and leave no room for ambiguity which can lead to error.) In healing we can read the body of the person we are working with by tuning into their energetic system. Whilst healing, we also bring their state of consciousness closer to ours, when we are well attuned with our ever-present higher source. (Ours should already be as close to that of 'God' or the source, or field, as is possible for our personal level of development.) So they feel touched by the pure peace that settles upon us as we work. As we further learn and develop, so we evolve further towards being more at one with that peaceful core. The only way to truly achieve this is with humility. There is very little room for ego in an unconditionally loving being. Ego power is surrendered to the more subtle power of being totally aware of who you are and what you are doing, and knowing the complete innocence in being in tune with the essence of life itself. You are even more responsible in this state. Yes, you still need ego to exist in the practical world, but it does not try to take you over, you remain heart centred.

We do all have part of this 'source' energy within us, for that energy is everywhere, but we tend to block it off, suppress it, deny it – due to the ways of our Western 'civilisation', yet we can choose to accept it and consciously develop it. I believe that any so-called fight against 'evil' is in fact a dissolving of this blockage against the 'Godliness' within us, which was often brought about by fear, and so needs to be conquered through love, which in turn brings us to love.

Yes, I do believe there are other sources of power, which can be dangerous, but these are at a lower level [plane / dimension]. This is undeveloped rough, and confusing power, whereas the 'source' energy is pure and fine and totally loving, and of a much higher frequency. Anyone who deliberately or carelessly uses other powers has been distracted by the ego and its self-centred motivations. Still we should not judge, only send them love. Love can dissolve anything if you can hold it steady enough in the face of whatever is happening.

People resist becoming fully themselves for all sorts of reasons, and only do themselves damage, and this is why they need healing on all the various levels from physical to mental to emotional to spiritual. Healing works at all levels of being. Once they can truly accept their healing then they will be back on the path to being themselves, which in turn then means that they can come closer to 'Godliness', or GOODLINESS. When we are truly being ourselves, we come as close to the source as we can be in that moment. I believe that healing can unblock or dissolve all problem areas and restore balance to the entire system. I believe that the emotional level causes most illness – we literally make ourselves sick through unbalanced responses to life. Being sick forces us to take time to pay attention. Hopefully we will look at the overall balance of our life and not just patch up symptoms, or we won't heal properly. We should learn to use mental tools to stop us from reacting in unbalanced ways, and to calm us so that we can function optimally. We mostly think too much, instead of being in the flow, which keeps us polished like beautiful pebbles in the stream of life, which is love, which is your 'God' or the 'Source', which is everything in its natural energetic state before being manifest.

I believe that the Holy Grail, Atlantis etc, are symbols of the perfection we seek. But this is perfection that cannot be found anywhere other than within ourselves. The sword is a symbol for the courage to undertake our personal journey (inward, as well as outward) and to cut our ties with anything we don't want. Merlin is the symbolic wise old man of the woods who helps us answer questions from within. He is simply one of many archetypes we can use to draw on hidden wisdom, which seems magical, but is really a communication with our own Higher Selves, which are linked with Universal Gnosis or Knowingness. These symbols exist in the collective mythical memory of man (such as that which Carl Jung spoke of), and have been used through the ages to help us come closer to ourselves.

I believe that we have everything we need within us to journey towards 'mastery', we only have to open ourselves to it. We can use spiritual energy, mysticism, and meditation to help us, or we can find our own way even without these. It helps if you spend time in the natural world and/or do work that helps others and feeds your soul, but again, even without these it is possible with simple love.

What does one strive for if one wishes to work towards 'mastery'?

1) BEING – in the flow you are happy without having to put any energy into creating that state, it just IS, no matter what.

In spiritual terms - this constant connection with the source is attained through the purple crown chakra (can also be seen as white) and brought into the heart (green, or sometimes pink). But you also need to stay grounded with the earth (red root chakra) and quietly and confidently balanced in yourself emotionally and mentally (yellow solar plexus), and in terms of vitality and sexuality (orange sacral chakra). Sometimes we can learn those lessons of the lower chakras along the way and then forget them again in the joy of attaining the pure crown link, but we need to remind ourselves to maintain them. In the higher centres, the light blue throat chakra should be constantly balanced to aid communication, and the dark blue brow is for intuition.

This state can also be achieved if you are simply immersed in nature or a balanced life, such that you do quite naturally feel at one with the life force.

2) LOVING – nothing can change this once you achieve a state of unconditional love, it just is, and stays that way no matter what. Again, in spiritual terms, this is through the heart chakra (the pink and green being like blossoming trees or flowers). On the way there, you may keep thinking you are there, but then you are tested and may go off track for a couple of days before returning, and each time this happens you incorporate new levels of understanding.

You can even send unconditional love to someone who may consider themselves your 'enemy', or to someone you saw on TV, or anyone who seems to need help, via pure thought / intention. Try to understand that even negative deeds are mistakes in many cases, and you can hope people might learn from them.

3) RESPECTFUL – I think we need to be able to respect everyone we spend time with for being who they are, to make unconditional loving easier to achieve. It is perhaps easier to keep one's cool with people one seldom sees as they don't touch your life so much, so the ones who are most around us often present the real challenges. It's a good idea to purposefully look for things you can respect in your parents, other family members, friends, partner, bosses etc, so that you can remind yourself of these anytime you feel a bit piqued with them!

4) KNOWLEDGEABLE / WISE – This knowledge comes from learning to know you deeper self and its connection with the universal source - that pure state of Gnosis. Wisdom is knowing how to use that knowledge – never misusing it, only gently being with it for the right purpose. The light blue throat (communication) and dark blue brow (intuition) chakras come into play here, though still linked with the heart.

NOTE - The top chakras are the ones that hold the 'Father, Son and Holy Ghost' type connection, plus sun, moon, stars, planets, water, and air or sky. I actually see a turquoise chakra opening up in people becoming healers, between the heart and throat ones, perhaps because we are starting to communicate with our higher selves. The root link with earth is a motherly one, but also a cleansing fire one which spreads upwards into the centre of vitality too, and the verdant green plant of the heart also reminds us that we truly need the mother energies as well as the father ones to survive on this planet. The lower chakras are more to do with our personal development before one is truly able to open the heart, which is the gateway to the higher ones. We have to move up the system, but we do still use the lower ones in our lives on this planet. The esteemed solar plexus yellow and sacral orange and root red are all fire or sun colours, and warm colours of leaves falling in autumn – which remind us to keep trust through the cleansing austerity of winter. Since we don't hibernate to recharge in winter, we should use it as a time of gathering our thoughts, writing, doing research, collecting ideas, and even catching up on indoor tasks. It's also a natural thing to eat more warming foods and enjoy being snug – nurturing ourselves – without getting fat. It's great to try to use the natural cycles instead of trying to resist them – and to actually celebrate them. The lower chakras, with their autumnal colours, sustain us from the ground up - they give us our vitality, our sexual and our physical energy for being and surviving here.

5) A 'master' HAS NO NEED – is like 'God'. If you are in that state of being where you have access to all knowledge and ability, then you have no need to try to control anything or anyone. You can also see that most things do not matter really.

6) A 'master' HAS NO EXPECTATIONS – people shall be as they are, things will be as they are in each moment. However, you do make choices, creating your own reality. If you are not fully aware then you make blind choices. A 'master' chooses to be who he is no matter what, and his choices reflect this.

7) A 'master' DOES NOT MAKE ASSUMPTIONS – there is always a way to turn assumptions around to make a mockery of what you assumed!

8) A 'master' DOES NOT JUDGE – everyone is on their own path - in the place they should be at that moment. If you accuse someone else of being judgemental, then you are judging them! Allow others to be as they are.

9) A 'master' TRUSTS – lives in the flow. Allow your existence to become fulfilled in a natural and unforced way. This does not mean that you don't do anything, it means that you are very steady in following your path and do not fret at it, but simply do what needs doing. You don't waste energy in fighting for your path, you just do it because you know the way you must go. You do not argue with others about this – you ask them to respect your journey, and promise in turn to respect theirs. This doesn't mean you can't work in partnership – there's usually plenty of room for this as long as each of you is fulfilled.

10) A 'master' IS UNLIMITED – in the flow there are no limits – love, abundance, time – it is all there aplenty. We should go ahead and experience the abundance available on this planet, to this physical body, as well as experiencing the higher emotional and mental planes. If we shut ourselves off from experiencing this abundance then it is going to waste. All that amazing creation should be joyfully celebrated. On the other hand we should also not be wasteful or destructive in the way we experience abundance. We should be respectful, thankful, and balanced about it.

11) DOES NOT WORK FROM EGO – working from ego is not being in the flow but being tied up in one's own agenda, and having ego investments in what other people think, in other words placing importance on one's self as separate from others, or on one's results (which is having a need for control, and expectations – see numbers 5

29

& 6). Working from ego can mean losing one's way pretty badly. If you find you are trying to control what other people do or think in any way, then you are working from ego. Not manipulating people does not mean you let people walk all over you - you still stand up for yourself appropriately, and remind people to be fair. You respect each other's freedoms and choices, and remind each other of trust if needed. If you act in fear then that is because you are trying to protect your ego. Once you realise that it does not need protecting, there is no further basis for such fear. Of course you can still discuss information and viewpoints, but always maintaining respect for the views of others.

12) A 'master' IS PART OF 'GOD' or the universal source - as 'God' or the source is part if him / her.

13) A 'master' DOES NOT TAKE ANYTHING PERSONALLY – if one is in the flow, then no one and nothing can touch you, you are unshakeable, because you KNOW. If you keep loving then you do not react to things irrationally. You know who you are, and what others say or do does not matter. What others think of you does not matter. There is no need for anger, each is on his/her own journey. There is also no need for forgiveness because there is nothing to forgive.

    A 'master' does not take things personally because he/she takes no offence and knows there is no judgement, and every event is a gift for him/her to learn from and redefine him/her self as his/her highest possible self in relation to that experience.

14) A 'master' IS – a Being of Light. KNOWS, ACCEPTS Grace – and is graceful. They also project that grace around the place.

15) A 'master' HAS NO RESISTANCE – what resists persists – lessons keep on happening until we accept the learning. Everything is meant to happen as it does, even if it means difficult lessons in the event. We know we can overcome anything as long as we do not step out of the flow – and become caught up in the knots (self-created) of angst. We know we can offer problems up and receive insight and answers. Usually things are more simple than we think!

16) A 'master' SERVES – after all everything is unlimited so we have gifts for all, in every moment we walk in the flow we spread the glow wherever we go. We do not need to perform any particular acts, just

BE who we are, be loving-kindness. 'God' or the source does not need us to do anything. 'He' or it knows we will ultimately return, however long it may take - thousands of lifetimes perhaps – but that is nothing as time has no meaning to the source of All – it does not exist as we measure it – there is only a perpetual NOW. If each person was like this there would be no wars.

17) A 'master' knows there is always enough TIME and always enough life. Yet a master uses these wisely, not procrastinating or wasting. Time is a process of moments, each now. Life is a process of BEING, once and again and again. Whatever happens is just another step in the process of evolution, and we love life for the opportunities it brings to experience and grow.

     'God' or the source - is life, energy, which never ends, only continues to be formed & re-formed & in-formed - gathering knowledge and experience of the infinite myriad of options and objects life brings – appreciating the infinite extent of creation and learning to create more, and letting the creations evolve. We are part of this - like the ebb and flow of the oceans, the sand in shifting dunes, the very stuff (stardust) of universes. As the words of the song *Woodstock* go "We are stardust, we are golden, and we've got to get ourselves back to the garden". The garden is of course another major symbol – our earth, Eden, the heart chakra, a place of creation and abundance. Heaven is not a place, it is a state of being - from within – when we are linked to everything – a state of grace.

18) A 'master' IS GRATEFUL – for the 'perfection' of each moment and all it has to offer. For everything he or she has, no matter how small.

19) A 'master' knows no such thing as a predestined future, only a chance to learn by sharing who we are in relation to each moment. There may be some things that are more likely to happen than others, but we retain choice, which is obvious when we are fully aware.

20) A 'master' knows there is no such thing as mistakes – only a chance to learn.

21) A 'master' has no more need for forgiveness as one who does not judge has no grudge to forgive – one who loves has already forgiven

others and themselves unconditionally along the way, and has no future need for forgiveness once they stop judging. If you are truly allowing each person to be as they are in each moment, then you are trusting that everyone is on their own paths and you have no personal need to try to influence that.

22) A 'master' has no fear, with all of this, what could there be to fear. Love dissolves fear. If we are not attached to a particular outcome we have no fear of not attaining that outcome. If we know that life goes round like the flow of a river following the shape of infinity, there can be no fear.

<u>Here's a song I just wrote</u>

Get out of your shell and go kiss the world
there's more than enough to see and learn.
Though some of it's tough, there's also love!

Your soul, your mind, and your body can burn
with the natural fire and delight of life
if you open your heart from where it's curled up tight.

So open your eyes to this amazing world.
You are the one - who asked to come
so don't keep your soul-self hidden any more.

Don't waste your chance to experience
and expand your consciousness
through all the tools that you are given here.

Come out of your shell, and dance at last!
You'll find so much you'll want to explore -
so be bold enough - to kiss the world after all.

*

"We are all vulnerable but do not fear this, just revel in the chance to experience that & know & grow beyond."
Joules

Are there such things as soul contracts?

If we accept for a moment that some people think there ARE such things, this allows me to explain what they supposedly are:-

Soul contracts are agreements we make in our pure spirit energy forms before coming into the physical body. We may decide we want to learn certain lessons for ourselves or fulfil a certain course of events. We then come into a situation where that can happen. We may choose our family and other people we will meet, beforehand, to learn certain qualities or tough lessons from, or we may choose other circumstances entirely. If you meet someone who you feel sure you already know, this may be due to them being one of these souls.

But another possible explanation for this is that you came down from a similar aspect of the source, as the energy divided down to coarser levels able to exist here. This seems to be borne out by my channelling sessions with The Beings of Light (in other books). I certainly have those feelings with people who turn out to be significant in my life. So called 'younger' souls may enter different levels of experience than 'older' ones, who may have already gone through several stages, and can often remember glimpses of them.

Perhaps such ideas are just a way of making situations easier to bear, and gives us some sort of logical approach to facing 'difficult' circumstances or people? (If it works, why knock it?)

A great friend will let you express yourself completely, whether it be in music, or speech, or love, and let you just be yourself, doing what you need to do on this earth. A great friend will also speak honestly with you about who you are if you need reminding to get back on track. And a good friend will also express appreciation of your qualities, thus affirming you. Hopefully you will be able to do the same for them. Perhaps you could deliberately bring such things into friendships that you want to flourish, but they do tend to happen naturally with people you feel you have known forever somehow, as if you've been round together a few times.

There are countless probable paths leading from every moment and it is our choice which ones we take. It is through these choices that we learn, and define who we are. Some paths may become more probable than others when a series of events take place but we can still change that. However, on the other hand, if we feel that we aren't in control of our lives then we are more likely to drift onto negative paths.

Our own thoughts affect where we go next. If you have

decided strongly on a particular course of events, then that is more likely to happen because of our focus on it. Just as if you are negative you attract more negative, and you attract the positive by being positive. A (genuine) psychic may see the stronger probabilities, but that does not mean they cannot be changed, it is up to us to choose whether to let that happen or not. If you choose to believe what the psychic has told you then you will focus on it and it will happen.

Seeing events in the 'future' of a country or of the world is different because an individual can do little to change that, apart from trying to warn people. Sometimes such events may be readable because they leave energetic shock waves that travel all around them in time. (I don't think we understand time very well yet, especially if we just see it as being linear {a Western limitation in logic} – what about waves, folds, or even loops, and radiations out in all directions & dimensions?) Some events may have been planned and thus would be in the sea of thoughts around us, so we could pick up on these intentions, in the same way as we often pick up on the intention of a close friend to phone or visit us, or dogs or (in our case) cats pick up on the moment a 'master' turns for home. (The cats come to meet us!) On a smaller scale, I have often received warnings to be careful, especially when driving, and have avoided several accidents, or other unpleasant outcomes, by responding appropriately to information given somehow about something up ahead or just around a bend.

It is important to be clear about what one wants to achieve. If you muddy the waters by not making up your mind and finding too many if's and but's and maybe's, then you interfere with your own hopes and plans. That is why sometimes it is also important to keep things to yourself for a bit, so that others do not muddy the waters for you unwittingly.

Part of why life coaching works so well is that a viable plan is put in place which totally focuses one's intention. (A good life coach can also help you identify what it is you might want to do, if you are not sure about this.)

Do we learn on behalf of the ALL that is, so that the collective ONE can evolve too?

I think I do believe that this must be true. As 'God' or the Stream of Consciousness is so perfect perhaps he/it cannot experience anything outside of itself, anything that is less than perfect. I mean, if our lives went totally perfectly we wouldn't learn anything would we, and so we would not evolve either, it would all just be as it was, continually.

So we come down through denser and denser layers until we are in the physical form, and we forget where we came from so that we can start to learn as if we were (only) separate, until we truly awaken and return – to seeing ourselves as part of the one-ness. Through this illusion of separateness we experience what a lemon is and how it tastes, what it is like to swim in the sea or walk in the woods, how a rose smells, how sunlight feels and looks on different surfaces, and so many millions of things, as well as experiencing the vast range of emotions stemming from interactions with other supposedly separate human beings.

This could also explain the myriad forms of life, all with different physical and other attributes, different abilities, and different experiences – plus different ways of responding to those experiences. While they are probably just representations of life spreading out, expanding creation, they do also maximise experience. So, if we are linked to the original stream of consciousness, doesn't it stand to reason that it would also expand through our experiences? I know it's already the all of everything, but it would continue to become more as the everything-ness increases.

The global level of collective consciousness can also expand as we bring new ways of thinking (and communicating) to it, instead of just using the old archetypal patterns – thus we can consciously bring in more peace, love, etc – as we do with our "Back to The Garden" open global group on facebook.

Why do 'bad' things happen?

People say that if there was a 'God' he would not let bad things happen, but surely it is only our limited judgement that labels them as 'bad'. Fears and chaotic thoughts can attract such events, thus if we manage to step back, we can learn from them. In any event situations arise that don't look very nice to us, but in my book "No Paradox....", I suggest that we have to have all possible 'sides' of the (multi-dimensional) coin apparent in the matrix that allows us to exist on this planet. If the stream of consciousness did not split out into every possible variation, then we could not truly experience life here – without hot there would be no cold, etc. So without polarities and gradations, there would be nothing to actually experience. Without contrast and comparison how would we measure our feelings?

'God' is not there to control events, but on the other hand 'he', or the stream of consciousness, can help us through developing our conscious thoughts. Asking for help is putting us in a situation of believing that it will make a difference... therefore it does. So we are back to our own thoughts influencing what happens... but also, if you are in the flow, the universal energy system will help keep you balanced as long as you allow yourself to be in it and not resist it. And if your mind, body and spirit are consciously in tune with that flow then so will your actions be - you are awake and will be guided to act in higher ways rather than simply react to situations or persons who are not yet in that flow.

If you are in the flow then you feel in control. You can direct your life the way you want it to be, by being the person you want to be. You can choose the experience of love, abundance, and happiness by believing that you are already that being experiencing that state of being. If you are steadfast then no other experience can change that. If you allow others to influence you then you are giving away your power to them – and thus still living in the illusion of separateness.

It is that illusion of separateness that leads us to judge and label things as 'good' or 'bad'. Yet that illusion of separateness is necessary for us to exist here, that illusion of the stream of consciousness having spread out into apparent strands, creating apparent polarities or opposites, is what gives us the framework within which to exist. Without that splitting out, there would be only the one stream from whence we all originated, and we could not be individually aware of any thing or experience. There would be nothing to compare anything against. What I am advocating is that we can live within that system and yet maintain an awareness that it is only a 'matrix' or construct, and therefore not allow ourselves to be dragged this way and that by reacting irrationally to various parts of it.

Reactions preclude balanced choices and therefore preclude real choice of who you are being and where you go from there. It's a bit like kicking yourself in the shins or cutting off your own nose to spite your face. I know – I've done it many times! Ouch! When one understands that everything that happens has a lesson in it then you do not need to fight against events, but let them flow and learn to view them differently, and make appropriate choices gently. This way nothing can really hurt you. People you meet once you are in the flow are people you are meant to meet and they too have lessons for us, or gifts. In every moment there are gifts, if we are aware enough to receive them – that is why each moment is called **the present** – and the more we learn the faster we evolve.

Tuning an engine or an instrument helps it to work better, as tuning ourselves does. We evolve as we fine-tune ourselves to the point of being able to live as a 'master', truly, constantly in the universal flow of life energy / love / abundance / not judging or assuming or needing, or taking anything personally – but knowing, trusting, and being in a constant state of grace all along our journey.

This also means moving away from the busy state of doing, into a state of being. Often, activity comes from the idea of a need to fight for survival, whereas once you are in the flow you trust that things will happen as they are meant to. This does not mean of course that you do nothing. It means that in each moment you choose to do what is clearly right for you, instead of rushing around in confusion trying to store up moments from the past or capture moments from the future, thus getting tied up in knots of anxiety which block our energy flow. We are happy now, we do not depend on something happening in the future in order for us to be happy, and we have let go of the past, and moved on. Either we have learnt the lessons from those moments that have gone before, or we have realised that it does not matter.

Time is abundant, as is love, and we can create anything, as we ourselves are unlimited in each moment as 'masters' in the flow if life.

We are aspects of the original creative life force, and we can create as it does, we can love, we can heal, we can do anything we dream of. Being in a state of Grace where you live and breathe that pure energy of existence, is blissful. It feels loving, it feels safe, it feels perfect. (I think some people need to see a 'God' as being like a person as that is easier to grasp than a stream of consciousness, but I note that 'Gods' represented as being wrathful, provide a useful method of controlling 'God fearing' citizens, whereas a pure stream of consciousness does not.) We see things according to our belief, which usually starts off being rather limited and then expands. However, children are often born wise only to have it knocked out of them by being forced to conform with our 'systems'. But things can shift back again to a greater awareness, maybe gradually, or maybe suddenly.

World events can shift the consciousness of many people at one time – 9/11 split people into those who were defensive, hated their 'enemy', and were angry, and those who moved beyond that, seeing a bigger picture of understandable human fallibility on all sides, and tuned into loving kindness, forgiveness, and a wish for peace. I personally witnessed, via my networking, many Americans and others making this shift within a few days after 9/11. Amazing!

The internet has also allowed a big shift – a sharing of information so that people can research events and think for themselves (instead of simply absorbing major media messages), and an allowing of global team-working for positive change.

I believe that the planet itself is evolving as well as all species upon her. Sometimes natural events cause shifts. Sometimes some species move ahead faster than others, like dolphins, then they seem to want to guide us, to awaken us to what they sense is happening.

I also believe that there probably are other universes and other beings, all evolving too. Perhaps there is a 'God' for each, or perhaps all are outposts of one infinite system. 'God' for me is, as ever, not a person or being, but a life force or creative universal energy, a vital source of all that is. Perhaps there is such a source for each universe – a system which creates and supports everything within it. Everything comes from this source and eventually returns to it. I've seen this ebb and flow in my visions and felt the umbilical suck and pull of life returning to Universe then back to life, like a 'God' breathing, even moving from one universe to another, or between matter / anti-matter.

I believe there are 2 energies at the core of human experience. These are not good and evil, but love and fear. Unconditional love opens you up to the flow of life and 'God'. Fear of falling from love (or of not obtaining it) denotes a misunderstanding of love. Love does not have to be fought for, it is simply opened to, and given - as well as received – a continual flow. Fear ties us up in knots so that the flow cannot go through and you are closed off to the vital life force. Fear of losing something (one perceives one needs) is often the basis of irrational human reactions, even just fear of losing control over someone (who is supposedly fulfilling a perceived need for you). But unconditional love simply shows itself, regardless of the circumstances. It does not need to control anyone or anything, it sets everyone free. And it does not need things in the same way either. If you are whole, you do not need to look to others to fill gaps in your being.

FEAR stands for False Evidence Appearing Real. I think that so far in my experience with all the illusions we have built, all the false beliefs, all the problems we have created – everything that stops us being real - stems from fear, which is of course a lack of true love.

Unfortunately unconditional love is generally not what religions teach – the idea that one religion is right and another wrong comes from fear – and causes war. The same thing happens when any lot believes they have more rights than another lot. Religious groups, by their own definition, live within a limited idea which excludes all other ideas. Any person or group of people who think their way is the only way and feel compelled to try to make everybody else believe their way - is actually acting from fear and a wish to control, restrict, and judge. The 'God' of religious organisations is put in charge of us, given power over us, and the leaders in the system enjoy more power than the masses, just like any other hierarchical system, all of which have the potential to be abused. These organisations generally do not act from unconditional love, which sets everyone free to be who they can be. Just as other organisations do not much like free thinkers, religions tend to condemn those who say they hold 'God' within their hearts, treating this as a blasphemous attempt to usurp 'God's' power, because they see it as a threat to their monopoly of it.

Because they are looking at 'God' from the premise that they are separated from 'Him', they do not understand the deep and natural, peaceful but joyous connection that does not usurp anything, but only loves. (I do however get that surrendering yourself to an external power can actually be another way of letting go of stress, or health or emotional issues, so it can be quite beneficial in the short term; and also religious gatherings can be quite social events. However, the fact that you are handing over your whole life might eventually become quite worrying if you think about it.)

There are exceptions of course. The word Namaste means "the 'God' (or spirit) in me recognizes the 'God' (or spirit) in you".

'God' is in everyone (whether we recognise that or not), and we are all linked by that, and each path to 'God' is merely another way, not something to be argued over. The ancient Sufi poet Rumi is (to me) a great one to read on religion and love.

The great universal source of all life cannot truly be divided into separate 'Gods', religions, or any other doctrine. All division is illusion. Those with ego based power know only too well how to divide and conquer.

Fear is a strong emotion, the energy of which draws that which we fear to us. What you resist persists, but what you look at dissolves. If you reflect only love to someone who is trying to harm you, they cannot continue. (You can even laugh at attempts to control you, but laugh gently, lovingly, not mockingly.) If you react in anger then you are feeding their power to influence you, to disrupt your state of mind.

I think that so called 'evil' people must be part of the same one-ness that we are, only they are blind to it and twisted by confusion. Even those who seem to be drawing on real power, must draw it from the 'All that Is' – but from a lower level than that of unconditional love. How can a 'devil' exist if it is not part of the 'all that is'? It could even be a part of us we made up to explain all the 'bad' things we do, or it could just be part of the overall apparent paradox.

If we are living in any illusion where we worship some thing, or being, that we fear and/or that gives us power, then that power itself must be limited, and we are limiting ourselves by placing ourselves under the control of that which we worship, rather than being a free and equal part of the All. Spiritual people generally do not obey or control, they try to live in symbiotic harmony with all around them. If they carry their light constantly within, then they are going to act with that light as their guide, because it is their personal link to the universal, and they know their own truth of being. If someone or something does "wind them up" then they must find ways of dealing with it, or choose to walk away, so that they can return to their equilibrium. (Perhaps it's a signal to move on from a job, or other arrangement, that's changed too much from what you chose to take on, or that you've outgrown. A clear understanding of the situation is important so that you can weigh up all the benefits against the negatives before deciding. Perhaps you can agree ways of adjusting that balance, or lay down certain boundaries, to enable you to continue?)

I am not saying there is anything fundamentally wrong with religion – it can serve a useful purpose in fulfilling the needs of many, providing a cohesive belief system for people to live by, plus a social network, and a support group too - if it focuses on love, rather than war! All I am saying is that it's a limited idea for people to live within, like any other of our constructs. If we are objective, we recognise this.

Each person or group of people have a right to have their own systems, so religion should never be forced on people, however, people living within each system tend to struggle to see outside of it enough to understand this.

The spirituality of oneness goes beyond religion in that it encompasses all beliefs and knowledge, and each person can blend with the 'All that is' to become a part of a cosmic whole. Everything can be seen in the light of this. We try to live in each moment as we truly are, experiencing life and love with joy, and seeing each experience, and person one meets, as a blessing brought to join us on our evolutionary journey, maybe for only a moment, maybe for much longer.

Colour outside the lines, live outside the box. Don't let anyone tell you what to do, or not do. Don't be afraid, listen to your heart.

Heaven is a state of being – of one-ness, and Hell is a state of being – lost. We simply need to live as we best define ourselves, find our own ways of being who we are in our world.

There is no requirement - only freedom of choice. We should not be judged if we are doing what we think best according to our perceptions at any given time.

Guilt should be discarded, moved beyond - what matters is who we choose to be in the next moment, given what we might have learned. We continually create ourselves anew.

Forgiving someone is a great way to show love, and forgive yourself too for the hurt you held onto far too long.

Take back the energy you have wasted on these things and reclaim your power to be your next best self.

Honour the past, but refresh, expand, renew, fulfil. Heaven is within us, always reachable.

A 'master' can always ask the same question : "Who am I?" and get the same answer in each moment no matter what is experienced: "I am love, I am like 'God' or the universe, I am happy, I have no need, no conditions, no requirements, no lack, no judgement, no assumption, I simply AM, yet there is nothing which I am not."

If we are still on the way towards 'mastery', we will keep changing our definition of who we are as we develop in relation to our experiences, until we reach this stage of steady assuredness, if we ever do!

"The process of Mastery is one of acceptance. It is a quiet embracing of what is. It is a non-resistance. It is a gentle walking into the moment, knowing that it holds for us, always, what is best for us all ways. Do you believe this? Then it is true."
Neale Donald Walsch

"We are consciousness examining and expressing itself so that it can become increasingly aware of its infinite capacity for being, creating, and evolving."
Joules

"Living in a cosmic ocean, singing sweet hallucinations, dreams of many worlds, all flowing into one… inner / outer mirrored love."
Joules

"We are the Universe — seeking truth."
Joules

"Consciousness is everywhere — let it fill you up."
Joules

As we become 'masters', do we find ourselves recreated anew in each moment as the same being we chose ourselves to be in the last moment, or do we continue to evolve?

I think we are always in a process of becoming – things about us are never constant, so why would we be, absolutely? I think we do go over and over things to become more and more sure of who we really are being in this world. Sometimes people sense the pure energy of one's being and choose to follow that message or example, so in that process we can also serve – the creator, or creative force.

When you are in a state of 'mastery' then you can be, and are, fully responsible for your thoughts. You would not have a bad thought by mistake that would damage someone. Therefore your thoughts become more and more a way of actually making things happen. You choose what will serve your highest self, which is also the one overall self.

"Try to forgive by trying to understand how it would feel to be in the other's shoes. If someone hurts you – ask them - "What hurts you so much that you would do this?" Listen to the answer and try to understand what is valid for them. They may have been fighting for your attention, but no one thinks of themselves as attackers, only defenders! So don't judge their ways, only set them free by giving them a chance to speak. You may both learn a lot from your kindness and courage in asking for the truth. But even if nothing changes, release it, remember that you both have a right to be who you choose to be. When we make judgements we're inevitably acting on limited knowledge, so ask if you seek to understand, or simply let them be!"

As Neale Donald Walsh also says, *"The biggest difficulty with a problem someone is facing is rarely the problem itself, but the fear that nobody else understands it".*

There is no such thing as right or wrong, there is only what works and what does not work, depending on what you seek to do, or be, or have. Deciding that something is right or wrong is being judgemental. It is seeing things inside a limited illusion. Humanity is very good at changing its basic values anyway when it suits us! For example, cigarettes kill, but it is judged as okay for companies to make money out of selling them, however it is judged as wrong to practice euthanasia. The greatest gift for all is free will. 'God' gives us this and then we act as if he didn't. We need to learn tolerance and respect for each other's choices and different paths.

"You yourself are your own obstacle. Rise above yourself." Hafez

I entrain myself (whenever I remember to)
by tuning in to higher frequencies
in the ether, in my soul, everywhere I go,
always accessible, always helpful
for obtaining a higher perspective
in a matter of minutes.

"Thou shalt wear trousers, but they shall fall half down
to teach humility over arrogance."
Joules

HUMILITY

I don't condone any idea of some people being better than others. People are just on different journeys, and all journeys are equally valid. There need to be people at all levels of thinking and ability for the "matrix" to work. Everyone will have their chance to evolve, when they are ready, whether in this life or the next, or the next!

Imagine if we were all rocket scientists, the world would come to a standstill - we need variety, we need the network of life, to be able to flourish. Our planet is filled with the most wondrous variety, marvel at it, appreciate it.

Never forget to be humble, for if you forget that one thing, then so much could be lost. "Pride comes before a fall", as they say.

You can't be a light and loving being if you are mainly driven by ego and pride. Being humble doesn't mean you cannot be great, you can be great and still be humble, there are many examples of such enlightened beings out there, look to them for inspiration.

And look to the dedicated millions who hold the basis of our network together too, every one has a unique part to play in the great web of life.

♡ ♡♡ ♡♡ ♡

As John Heron from New Zealand said in a talk in Wales on the theory of co-counselling: *"All negative behaviour is entirely due to positive human potential being interfered with, primarily due to emotional pain, and aggression is reactive to frustration and repression of this positive. A negative self image restricts and distorts behaviour, and maladaptive coping mechanisms cause patterns to continually be misapplied."* He goes on to say that the three root causes of human distress are ignorance, social oppression, and natural disaster, and that the skills for survival and for personal and social development all have to be acquired through learning. He also says there is a sort of internal ignorance – being a form of amnesia, a forgetting of who we really are, which is a divine being with limitless capacity for expanded awareness and charismatic abundance. He says that somewhere in our beings we know this but suffer the angst of having forgotten, so that awakening and inward remembering is the paradigm shift that is needed in co-counselling. He says that this opening generates a higher frequency energy in the psyche which transmutes distress.

I agree with all of this, and am also pleased to have read and responded to an excellent paper by the National Youth Association on how to bring spiritual development into Youth Work, which was all published as a booklet. This very much coincides with what we hope to do primarily via our "Transitions into Adulthood" workshops. I have experience of social work with young people, youth work, and schools work, as well as being a counsellor for families and children, a healer, a life coach, a creative and spiritual tutor, and a writer, and I would personally love to give young people the tools for spiritual development, mixed in an acceptable way with practical exercises and logic.

"The human soul travels from law to love, from discipline to freedom, from the moral plane to the spiritual plane." - Tagore.

You know that feeling of invincibility you sometimes get, especially when young and testing yourself – well that could be because we actually know deep down that we are indeed eternal. We come into this world to live a life, to experience it, from somewhere else, some other plane, but we are programmed by all around us to deny or forget this – until one day we remember again.

That feeling of blissful reconnection with our source can be invoked through nature, beautiful writing or art, any detailed craft or work of discovery or personal dedication, meditation or other mentally balancing practice, or even through religion – if there is a pure communion, not some pretence of it).

But we should not yearn to return too soon, as some do, we should accept that we have come here for the duration of each life, and revel in the chance to learn and grow on this splendid planet. We can draw a deep sense of being-ness, peace, and love from this connection which will sustain us through any trial.

Once nurtured, this becomes stronger than any other connection, so of course our relationships here are most joyful when they allow us the personal freedom to spend time developing and celebrating that connection. Our deepest friendships form with those companions we can share such time and experiences with – discussing, meditating, immersing ourselves in nature, or creating our music, art, written or other works. Our journeys here are voyages of discovery, opening out the wonders within and all around. What better companions could we have than those who are able to fully share in such delights with us?

Innocent and Joyful
I take your hand
For I know you judge not,
You simply understand.

You are my companion
On this voyage of discovery,
Singing sweet soft music
To the universe inside of me.

I listen to the silence
And yearn to be more me,
Swimming in the sea of myself
- learning eternally -
finding out where the rocks are
and smoothing them into sand.

A little more on INTENTION

It seems to me that intention really is paramount. If someone does something through ignorance or lack of awareness then it is perhaps easier to forgive them "for they know not what they do". People learn from their own experiences, including mistakes, so hopefully all progress at their own pace. Sometimes it is possible to gently point out an anomaly in behaviour for example, but we can't go round preaching to people as to what we think they should do! We need to rather be aware of our own behaviour and try to live according to what we think – "be the change we wish to see in the world" or "show rather than tell". Positive intention, even if mistakes are made, shows purity of heart.

Negative intention, like when someone purposely goes out to hurt, deceive, rob etc, is harder to forgive. However, even the rich and powerful who have deliberately led us like sheep through a contrived and false history of our own civilization, seem to think that they have some sort of right to do this. Stories are passed on down their families about their birthrights etc, and certain behaviours taught, so they tend to follow as their ancestors have. Only a few are disgusted enough to break the cycle and behave differently, just as only a few who have been abused are strong and aware enough to not become an abuser themselves. We need to try to understand that people behave within the context of what they have learned. If such people become aware that this is not desirable behaviour, and wish to change it, then they really deserve support. However, there are some who pretend and deceive, so we should not be taken in too easily.

There are almost inevitably setbacks or lapses in the process or cycle of change for anyone, but support should remain steady regardless, to just quietly encourage them to get back on the wheel when they are ready to do so. It is a huge and positive challenge to break habits instilled in one's early years. Self awareness, at least enough to accept that there is an issue, is always a necessary prerequisite to successful change. We can't just expect people to change if they are not aware of the need to… and that has to mean them actually wanting to change, not just someone else saying they should.

It is always our own intention that moves us forward in personal development too.

We can choose to make it our intention to truly experience our lives, which in our maturing awareness, we then realise also fuses with ALL experience, so we accept the responsibility of that with humility.

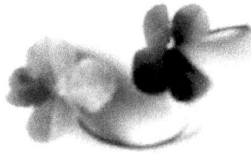

A little mantra

Peace is coming to my heart.
Peace is coming to the world.
We are all connected to
the Universe within
where peace resides.

Peace is filling up my heart.
Peace is filling up the world.
We are all connected to
each other through our hearts
where peace resides.

Peace resides within my heart now.
Peace resides within the world.
Peace resides within my heart now.
Peace resides within the world.
Peace is everywhere.

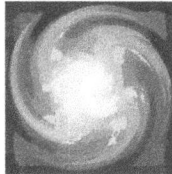

A brief simple but powerful meditation, using your intention to help others.

- Sit comfortably and relax. Repeat the word relax to yourself as your breath deepens and slows. Let go of tensions in all your muscles, moving down your body from top to toe, gradually, until it is all gone.
- Now open your heart to love. Repeat (all or some of) these words to yourself while you feel it open like a flower to the loving rays of the source – love, pure, relax, innocence, accept, forgive, love, compassion, gratitude, freedom. Add any of your own you fancy.
- Now envisage people you wish to help, one by one, and send them this heart light with your intention and repeat the words again for each of them. Add any words that seem appropriate and/or repeat the ones that seem most appropriate as often as you wish. See them lighting up and smiling as you do it. Move on from one person to the next at intervals that seem right, until each is done.
- Now, ensure you continue to accept love to renew yourself.
- When you are full and glowing, give thanks, and return gradually to your day. Have a drink of water please. It helps process / cleanse.

Lovelight

*From my poetry collection "Sacred Selves" and previously published in
the Region 2 (UK) Newsletter of the National Federation of Spiritual Healers.*

Sunshine,
Solace, splendour
Slipping inbetween
Slenderly reaching in
Tenderly inbetween your atoms
Seeing the shining within…
Bringing the sourcelight, lovelight,
To mix with it,
Blending, easing, believing,
Balancing, giving.

Lovelight,
You are complete.
Lovelight,
Thank you for your gift.
Lovelight,
Each of us can be it….
Reach for it, add to it,
Transmit it.

Lovelight
Growing in our hearts,
Minds, bodies, souls…
The universe without
Swirls in…
And out again…
With its warmth
Dancing, smiling, shining.
Glorious lovelight
Thank you!

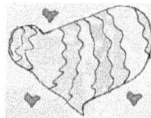

Looking back at 'Mastery'

A lot of the thinking related to being a 'master' may seem impractical in the real world where we have to survive as practical beings. We cannot just retire and meditate all day.

But we can learn to exist in both worlds or at both levels at once – we can call on the parts of us we need to do the practical things, and yet still be aware of the other levels. We can integrate everything we know and do into an overall balanced way of being.

We are both individuals and interconnected. We can live our lives, and always be aware of the wider perspective. If we can keep one eye on some of these ideas until we integrate them into our being, then we can keep learning, keep journeying, towards our own ultimate sense of being who we fully can be, as well as being part of everything.

Perhaps 'mastery' is simply accepting that we are part of the mystery.

"Enlightenment is not about cocooning one's self,
but about integrating more fully with both your self and life."
Joules

"Dance your soulful path
and you shall know the magic
of your mind and heart
and all the beauty laughing
to fill your rising self."
Joules

*

FURTHER DISCUSSION

What might happen after death?

Well, I have been lucky enough to remember being somewhere else before here. When I was a child I remembered being in a sort of room, almost like a classroom situation, where we were learning stuff, like what the laws of physics *really* were. When I was very young I used to say things like "Our laws of physics will change, they do not understand Time and Gravity yet," and "Magnetism is more important than they seem to think." (I soon learnt to shut up though as 'grown-ups' didn't like it.)

Unfortunately I don't remember the details of the lessons, but sometimes when someone says something, usually about a newly discovered point, I say "Oh yes," as if I vaguely remember that bit now. I don't have a great mind for details, nor do I understand things like higher mathematics, but I'm a bit of an 'all-rounder' and kind of get a conceptual grasp of a lot of stuff. I also often have ideas that turn out to be significant – these might come from simple observations of nature, or from seeing the patterns in the very tiny and the very large (atoms to galaxies for example), or from watching a programme that raises questions for example about our bodies and minds, space, dimensions, black holes, etc. Sometimes they just come from visions when meditating. (I wonder if someone who knew what they were doing had cross-questioned me as a child, if I could have remembered more. As I know from dowsing, asking specific and relevant questions does tend to bring clear answers.)

Anyway, I feel lucky to remember being elsewhere because I have never been afraid of death itself, mostly because of this (only of possibly suffering beforehand). The cycle of the seasons and of plants etc, seems to bear out that our lives might also go in cycles.

Later on I realised that it wasn't just learning from some teacher, it was also a sharing, a kind of telling of our stories, with everyone sharing what their experiences on earth had been like, remembering details, learning more fully. Maybe we were like scouts sent out to check out the lie of the land – see if it was safe – decide what we could do – carry out a role? It was certainly as if we were going out to do a project, then returning to discuss them, before the next stage.

Later still, in fact late on in the process of writing my books, I realised that our experiences on earth might not be so much about just experiencing the vast variety of creation on behalf of the one stream of consciousness, but also more about us continuing to evolve after death.

Perhaps we do not just return to the one-ness like a drop of water returning to the ocean, but still retain some individual identity? This must be the case if I remember being in a 'classroom' situation.

How about it just being another level of consciousness? In our lives now, we have to return to periods of unconscious sleep for renewal….. our waking lives depend on it. Then we step up another stage when we become fully aware and live our lives so that we are directing the 'dream' we live in, rather than just going along with whatever happens. Again, the existence of our fully aware selves depends on there still being a practical self - we can't just be fully immersed in our spiritual side all the time, we have to use the more practical levels to exist here. So how about death then being like just another stage of awakening, when we don't need to survive physically here any more, but we continue to learn as spiritual beings? I don't know where we would be exactly, but maybe that's because we don't understand how we could exist outside of the physical… We might not need to actually be anywhere in particular, or we might just be in another dimension. Perhaps our lives there somehow depend on us returning to the physical life every so often – a series of blinks in time?

All the states of dream to full awakening are nested upon each other, we need to be in each one to know we are waking up to the next. If we just stayed in the spirit, then perhaps we would forget the lessons we had learnt from our sojourns here, and need to be reminded every so often. Perhaps guides and 'ascended masters' are the ones who have done it so often that they never forget, and can be relied upon to help others remember.

Here is another Tagore quote: *"Death is not extinguishing the light; it is only putting out the lamp because the dawn has come."*

Our dream personas are many, but they are chaotic, we can find ourselves being any old weird thing in any old weird situation, but sometimes we can learn from them. In physical life we also exhibit many personas so that we can fit into different roles and situations, but perhaps not as many as when we dream, and we are able to choose them, and when and how we use them. As we mature we use less

54

personas as we are able to settle into being who we really think we are, and worry less about what others may think of us. We have probably chosen to narrow down our roles to help us do this, for example having chosen to give up working in a job you did not truly love in order to focus on something you do, having chosen your partner and close friends and activities to fit in with who you are choosing to be. You are not swayed by peer pressure any more, and don't feel you have to yield much to other external pressures either.

After we die perhaps we finally become our fully true integrated selves? Or perhaps there are further stages, like if we forget the lessons of our journeying, and become confused or even stroppy, then we may have to journey further before we can become steady in ourselves? Perhaps we all return, or even go elsewhere. to try different sorts of journeys with slightly different lessons? Perhaps that is why some people, including myself, seem to remember bits of other lives. I have never set much importance on these other lives though, they don't seem relevant to me now.

I think perhaps that there is a problem for some people if their spiritual self is not properly seated in its body, and they need help from a healer or someone who understands this, to stabilize and ground them here. This can happen through shock (dislodgement), or perhaps from always thinking too much about wanting to be somewhere else (disconnection), maybe because they have some faint memory of being somewhere 'better'.

I think that we do need to see our lives here through properly, otherwise we will probably only find that we kind of have to do them over…. We probably meant to come here to learn or do something particular, so it is better to try to find out what that is and make the best of it.

Perhaps our experience of different lives and all the variety therein might actually validate and facilitate the continued and further expansion of consciousness itself? If so, then this would be particularly relevant if one was both creating and evolving in each life.

AWARENESS - Everywhere and Nowhere

Perhaps our awareness is always present everywhere yet nowhere. You can't put your finger on where it is – it isn't inside our heads, it seems boundless. We say we are coming from our hearts when we mean that we are not confused by the convolutions of our minds, but our awareness isn't there either. **Everything I am seems to be inside my awareness, rather than my awareness being inside of me....** My thoughts, my sensations, my body, my experience – all are inside awareness. My life arises and unfolds within awareness. My world arises within awareness. Awareness contains the appearance of everything – the flow of life forms arising and returning, the existence of stars and planets evolving through cycles. I am a character in the dream of awareness, but I can also become one with the awareness that is having this dream – being conscious of being conscious, and thus being able to consciously evolve, deliberately affecting the dream I am having of myself and my life. So our awareness is like a bubble of consciousness in the river of consciousness, and the rest of us exists inside that. Of course, we mostly only awaken gradually to such a concept.

As for where I exist when my physical body dies – everywhere and nowhere – I am never focused in any one place but I am wherever I wish to be. I can even spread myself around a bit, helping someone here, learning something there.... I have no physical limitations any more.

As my awareness here on earth, I can be an agent for change. States of consciousness are catching, so we can spread more awareness. Consciousness crosses all boundaries, so anyone can get it.

Consciousness takes us from nature to nurture. We have tried many things, many ways of living, and become disillusioned with them, but our journey will eventually take us beyond all those.

As more of us become able to consciously evolve our consciousness, not only do we become compassionate and understanding, but we are liberated from the collective dream which keeps us stuck in old stuff. So you can bring in the new, you can help create things the way you want them to be. What do *you* want to do with your potential while you are here?

STREAM

Humanity is a dream of itself!

We see the dream according to
What channel we switch on –

Despair, destruction, fear, chaos,
In the news and papers and city streets,

Or joy of nature, creation, art,
Living in bliss & thankfulness.

Here, here, here
We are now urgently
Feeling, needing, making
Ourselves become true beings,
Experiencing, awakening -

Dancing to the sounds of trees
And stones and slow minutes
Ticking in our hearts and bones -

Dancing to sun rays of hope,
Ice rays of clarity, skies
Full of dream shaped clouds.

You and I run through the days
With the woods and oceans
And animals and owls all calling
Out to us to become like them,
To breathe the rhythms of earth
Back into our blood to survive
Like wolves howling and feasting -
Thus to become more of ourselves,
And live in less confusion.

We are alive in all our layers
Of self and selflessness -
Individuals becoming One.

We are spinning in the cosmos -
Tiny, yet great as our God,
Filled with all the particles
Of knowledge in existence,

Filled with all the moments
Of past and future joined -
In each eternal moment -
Lifted on a rainbow singing,
Chests filled with love
And wisdom of complete innocence.

We are angels just like the rest
Of our brothers and sisters,
We are artists streaming
Our colours into the world
Where birds and flowers and butterflies
And cats, are our companions.

We are everlasting, perfect,
Transmuting, being
The sons and daughters
Of our Father, and Mother, Beloved.

If we succumb to denial, we negate;
But if we bless and create,
Then we grow into giants,
Timeless and accomplished,
Spreading our hearts all over the place,
Forgiven automatically.

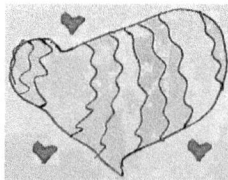

DREAMER

I am obsessed with joy of life,
What it means to feel and be here.
I am possessed with a curious need
To celebrate the wonders I observe.

I am a saxophone wailing in ecstasy,
I am a paintbrush laying down paint,
I am a lyricist making soul sounds
With words and notes to express visions.

I am an enchantment myself enchanted.
I am the dream and the dreamer dreaming.
I am the peace of the mountain, the woods, the desert.
I am the peace of the soul within all souls expanding.

I am the peace of the prayer within
That is everywhere mirrored and repeated,
Like the sky reflecting in the oceans,
Like the fire of earth repeated in the heavens.

I am love, and am beloved.
I am anointed by the hands of the anointer.
I am appointed by the original creator to create,
To pass on the holy whispers I hear.

To be one of many returning
With hearts full of blessings and tears,
With stories of what it is like
To feel, and be, a dreamer here.

universal Love

Meditation is one of the most important elements of spiritual development.

On www.radiance-solutions.co.uk/essenceguides.htm - there is a full MEDITATION GUIDE. I do cover brief details of meditation in various guides, but the meditation one itself covers a vast range of techniques in depth. (Intro / Basic Principles / Energies & Breath / First Techniques / More Techniques / Advanced Techniques).

You can also use Meditation for Subtle Activism purposes, which we do in our Back to The Garden Globally linked facebook group, to plant positive thought seeds into the collective consciousness, such as for Peace, Love, Healing, etc.

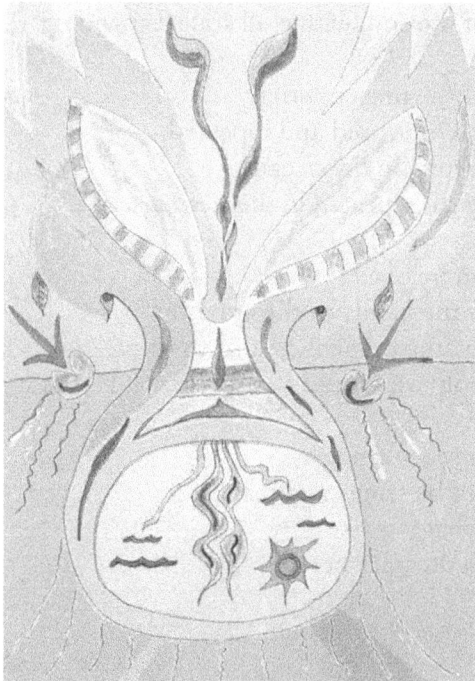

I am including some relevant
ARTICLES:

How to use Meditation to send out Peace, Love, Healing, etc. (Subtle Activism)

As a healer, meditation teacher, and writer, I thought I had better put my skills together and write a brief guide on how to do this for the members of our "Back to The Garden" facebook group specifically, but also to share more widely.

Part of the purpose of the group is to meditate during any of the suggested time-slots to link up around the world with others doing it at the same time, and send out waves of positive thoughts and wishes to help create the changes we wish to see in the world. I have recently come across a term that people seem to be using for this – subtle activism.

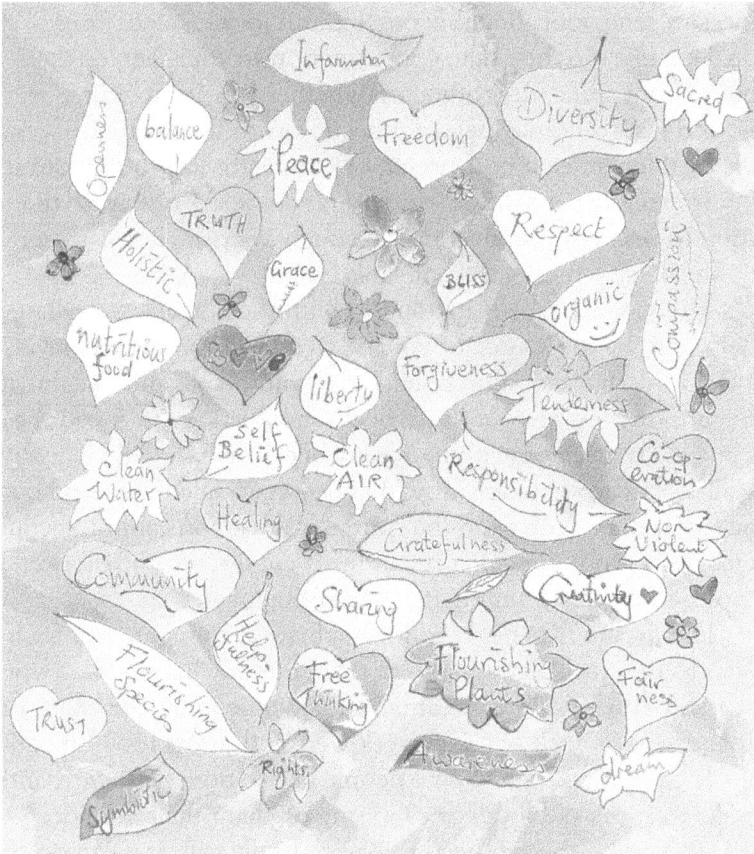

Anyone can do simple meditations by taking a few deep breaths and then allowing yourself to relax and breathe gently, focusing on the breaths and letting your mind become still. If you have trouble relaxing, it can help to begin with some simple exercises to release stress from your body, such as you might do to warm up for any sports session. If you have trouble with your mind chattering at you, just pretend you are laying each thought aside on a shelf and then continuing. You can also focus on a candle, flower, crystal, whatever you like if that helps – real, or in your mind. As you become more relaxed your sight tends to go slightly out of focus, so don't try to keep it sharp, just allow your eyes to soften and close.. Just relaxing like this regularly is very good for you, but we need to go a bit further to meditate for our purposes.

Once you are relaxed you need to get yourself into a state of readiness to send your thoughts out without losing any of your personal energy. So, first take your attention to your feet, or the bottom of your spine, depending on whether you are standing or sitting, and just feel (imagine) a connection with the earth (as if you are literally earthing an electrical circuit, or you might like to think of it as rooting yourself like a plant in our natural home). Just having the intention to make the connection is enough to create it, trust your ability, we all have these inherent skills.

The second stage is to connect with the universe, or whatever you believe to be the source of your power, God, angels, whatever, it all works. Ask that this source send energy into you, and imagine it coming into the top of your head, neck, shoulders, or into your heart. Continue to sit quietly breathing for a while, just feeling the energy going all around you. Know now that however much you send out, it will be replaced directly from the source, so that you cannot become depleted, as it is not drawing on your own energy, which you need to keep yourself well, it is simply flowing through you.

Finally you may begin to form whatever thoughts you wish to send out to the world, and just send them out in whatever way works best for you. It could be a stream, or it could be in little packets, or like leaves and seeds on the wind, even flowers and hearts too. Sometimes it helps to see the colours. Some people like to do this silently, and some like to speak out loud, or even sing or chant their intended messages. You don't even need to be physically still, you can do this whole thing while dancing or walking.

Once you are done, just return your focus to your breathing, and gradually become aware of your surroundings until you feel you are back to your normal waking state. Rub hands and feet if it helps. Move slowly to start with, and have a drink of water.

The trick of using altered states of consciousness such as in meditation or healing is not to try too hard, don't force it, just be gentle, and it will come naturally as you practice.

An added tip perhaps is to try using affirmations to get you even better prepared for sending out your messages. Once you have done the parts about grounding yourself to the earth, and connecting with the universe etc to receive energy, you can increase the sense of the energy coming into you by using affirmations such as : "I love. I am loved". Breathe deeply and smile as you feel the energy coming in. This is not love as in a romance, it is a deep two-way connection with the earth, and with the universe or your God, so that you actually become one with it all and you ARE love. It fills you up with strength and security, and knowledge that you are safe to participate fully in life, including sending out beautiful energy to the world. You can imagine pink flower and new leaf green colours too if you like, as those are the heart energy colours, so the visualisation will enhance the affirmation.

"You are the Universe – that's why it shines!"
Joules

To stay protected & energised during energy work, or anytime we are giving of ourselves to others (such as when on stage):

You can imagine a gentle golden bubble around you, with a soft membrane for the energy to easily be able to flow through, in both directions. Set your intention to be that whenever you give out energy, you receive nurturing energy in turn from the earth and universe to sustain you. You can also choose / stipulate when and where you send it out, so that people (in a shopping mall, for example) can't drag on it without your permission. It also protects you from other people's negative energy as it only allows positive energy in.

* * * * * * *

Free Thinking - Helping our Young People to Think for Themselves

In response to a blog about our young people self harming despite their parents trying to do everything right, and questioning if there is too much stress with lots of homework and other things they have to do – another person wrote that young people these days seem to be given things on a plate and organised too much. I made a further response to this:

Most people I know of my generation did have very bad things going on when they were kids, but somehow we were tough enough to deal with them, although they do still affect us, obviously. We never expected to be given things on a plate, we were brought up to think for ourselves, and to be versatile, and figure out our own ways of coping, and of getting where we wanted to be eventually.

Yes, children now are often organised so much – to fit into a system – but it is becoming obvious that there are things wrong with that system, so perhaps we should be helping our young people become more able to cope with challenges and changes instead of channelling them into specialised paths quite so much.

By the way, we had 2hrs of homework every day right through high school – because I was boarding, there was no choice but to go to the homework period between supper and lights out – not to say that I actually DID homework though – I mostly wrote poetry!

I used to swim 50 Olympic lengths before school and before dinner every day and do long distance running – but it was all very definitely MY choice to do these things.

I think I still had some time to muck about with my friends, but I only got to see my parents one weekend a month from age 11.

When I was home, I used to wander about in the wilderness most of the time though, so it must have been when I was very young that the free thinking and versatility stuff was instilled in me – unless I was just born that way.

There is a lot more I wanted to say though….

We know that giving kids things on a plate tends to make them self centred and less able to cope, yet this still happens. Perhaps society makes us feel we have to keep up appearances by providing endless provisions and activities….. but surely this can become too much like a competition – stressful for all.

We also know that it is better to spend quality time with our kids than to farm them out all over the place, and stress everyone out with hectic schedules; but yet again, we find ourselves doing this.

'Love' so often becomes a sort of 'cupboard love' which depends on visiting relatives or friends giving gifts or providing really fun days out, where the money spent on them seems to be valued more than the time spent with them - so it also teaches them to be devious, aiming to gain more and more of this false value in the absence of what really matters.

This can especially apply when couples have separated – the children can soon learn how to get things from each parent by turning it into some sort of competition if you aren't careful. If one parent, or a friend, decides not to play this game, they can find themselves 'dropped' just like that.

And yes, children are pressurised so much – to fit into the system, study hard, get a job, get a mortgage, have a family, accumulate things, and continue the cycle into the next generation. Do we ever question whether there could be another way – of not being slaves to the 'system', which we can easily see has its problems if we stop long enough to think.

So many people are not really thinking though, because in their limited spare time they seem to get sucked into TV - which tells them a carefully concocted version of reality that's very different from the real thing (newspapers too), or the pub – where they can numb their brains with drink and superficial conversations, or more business deals.

I suspect that some of our young people are having trouble understanding why we go on round and round in these meaningless circles, and this could be a source of much emotional distress to them.

When I was a teenager my poems were all about the terrible things humanity was doing to our natural world, and I know for sure that a lot of youngsters are very concerned about these sorts of issues. Even those who have an outlet for their feelings, such as writing poetry or writing and playing music, still struggle with the huge chasm between their understanding, and the world where people seem to be switched off, just working and drinking and acting as if the most important thing on earth was to be rich enough to both socialise and compete with people who have the same priorities.

Basically the 'system' gives the message that if you comply you will be given some of the 'sweets', just the same as spoilt kids – and once you start going down that road it is very hard to turn back, so you end up turning a blind eye, and doing all sorts of compromising things to ensure the sweets keep coming – particularly if you have now got a partner and kids to answer to if the supply stops.

Have you ever asked them though, what they really think, do you actually know?

Not everyone wants to be like that. Many young people are much more grown up and aware than that. If we don't encourage our young people to think for themselves, seek alternatives, or at least let them know that we accept, maybe even support, their need to do so, then they are going to feel very trapped, and also probably worried about disappointing us. Or of course, they may feel alienated from us.

Those benefiting from our current systems are not our young people at all – unless of course they really are brainwashed enough to want to be the next big business magnate – and if that is the case then we had better ensure they realise just what a corrupt and disgusting world that currently is, and try to help them find courage to at least do things in some new way.

Our 'system' perpetuates cronyism & specialism rather than independence & versatility, which means that you then tend to rely on others to provide the services and things you cannot do or produce yourself, and thus are relying on the continuing system whether you like it or not. It also expects you to do as you're told. We tend to be left thinking that we can't break out of it, but this isn't really true at all.

In fact, once the oil runs out, we will probably have to survive at more of a local level anyway, so we need to all be learning to be more versatile really.

However, if we went off now and did our own thing, or local community thing, then the big boys of the banking and business world, and the governments, wouldn't be making any money out of us, so they are constantly seeking more ways to shackle us and herd us dumbly forwards. While globalism is great in some ways, it can also be dangerous in that it could make us easier to control.

They want to keep us deeply entrenched, with our mortgages and other debts, our taxes and other commitments. But they also keep quietly adding more rules, regulations, restrictions, and requirements, to tighten the hold – to be able to take more from us and to stop us from doing much for ourselves, while also making it harder for us to do anything about it. Many of these threaten our freedom and our health.

They also want to keep us blindfolded, concealing the truth about just how incredibly awful they have been in their manipulation of events in their attempts to grab everything of value, control the world, and leave us to rot, because of course, they are afraid of retribution.

However, most people, and organisations, who are awake to what has been going on are quite spiritually mature, and are more interested in putting things right than in retribution or revenge. We just want to see everybody in with a fair chance of survival – with our freedom and health intact. We want to find sustainable ways of living, helping each other, and yet continuing to be our unique selves, and continuing to evolve consciously into a species capable of living in harmony - with our brothers & sisters everywhere, and with our mother earth.

So let's reassure our young people that we are prepared to go for this, or at least enable them to do so. Let's talk about it in families – there should be no taboos. Let's give them something to identify with, hope for, and help carry through. It's not the first time that we will be making some big changes, as history will show, so they had better believe we are capable of it. There is already so much good stuff going on that they should take heart from that too. Thankfully the internet has proved to be an amazing tool for sourcing information and co-ordinating efforts. Let's do this – let's pull this team together now.

Our website is www.backtothegarden.org.uk and our
"Back to The Garden" facebook group is open for anyone to join,
We are building links to useful sources of information & inspiration,
and co-ordinating global meditation link-ups for positive input into the
collective consciousness – the compost bed from which our new
garden will grow.

BEING REAL – John Lennon - in the Collective Consciousness

I started looking up John Lennon quotes on Goodreads – which helped inspire me to write this article. I only realised a day later that it was the anniversary of his tragic death – when I saw that a lot of my friends had also been looking him up and replaying his music. I don't think it was just a co-incidence that I made that connection, I do think that his spirit is still very much with us in our attempts to find better ways of being at peace with ourselves, and living more in harmony with the planet.

As I co-administrate a facebook open group called "Back to The Garden" some of his quotes were particularly relevant – such as "I'm not really a career person; I'm a gardener, basically." Also, "The thing the sixties did was to show us the possibilities and the responsibility that we all had. It wasn't the answer. It just gave us a glimpse of the possibility." Our group is already named "Back to The Garden" because of the 60's song "Woodstock" which says "We are stardust, we are golden, and we've got to get ourselves back to the garden". Our aim is to share information to help us try to live sustainable lives by creating supportive local communities, and to participate in global meditation link-ups to help influence the collective consciousness towards achieving this. We also share our creativity to help express our ideas.

My article shows why I think John is such a great example to us all – of how to truly be ourselves – although obviously he wasn't perfect either….. none of us are infallible.

John Lennon was such a thoroughly REAL person. His quotes reflect all sides of human nature, from the sad and withdrawn, to the desperately painful, to the angry, to the loving and celebratory, and from the arrogant to the humble, as well as from the serious to the exuberant humour-filled sheer absolutes of expression. We all have many sides to our nature but we tend to try to pretend that we don't, mostly because we are afraid to show some of it. Does society make us think that if we remain on a bland even-keel we are more agreeable to others? Surely we are more interesting if we share what we truly feel? It's perfectly possible to be honest without being horrid. Why can't we just accept all of it and be this real? Okay, we don't all need to be huge public characters, but we can be quietly firm about who we are and how we choose to be.

Another quote of John's which is staggeringly beautiful in its stark honesty is "When you're drowning you don't think *I would be incredibly pleased if someone would notice I'm drowning and come and rescue me.* You just scream."

If you are facing a period of 'depression', why not allow that to simply be, for a while? I generally have 3 days of it every now and again. I learnt from a very early age to manage it. You could say it was artistic temperament, but it isn't just that – we all have natural cycles energetically and physically, which affect us emotionally, and I believe we are better off listening to these than trying to deny them. (Of course, you should look after yourself with good nutrition, exercise, and the right amount of sleep, because imbalance in these areas can exacerbate or even trigger such periods.)

Basically I give myself permission to let it happen and actually explore it – I write or paint myself through it. I don't do anything I don't want to – I just live with it. Okay, so I don't usually publish what I've written at such times – but I do learn from it – and I am well aware that I am processing emotion, dealing with it – not trying to suppress it. I know that after the 3 days it will go again because I have given it the space to play through. Often I make positive changes in my life after these stages – so they are like transition phases. I seem to gather strength and insight from actually allowing them to really work through, and somehow grow from the experience. Perhaps by allowing the darker side its space, I then get recompense by gaining access to more of the light, because sometimes it is straight after one of these periods that I produce my best work.

Maybe if we look at it as if we are like snakes shedding skins so that we have room to grow some more, we could learn to process these phases naturally, we could all deal with them. Maybe they wouldn't hang around then – we could trust ourselves to get through them – not let them overwhelm us, or leave us stuck half in half out – we could go into them fully and come out the other side. I think it is healthy to allow ones-self to honestly explore all sides of your nature, as that is probably the only way you can truly get to know and trust yourself. I think that is why I love John Lennon so much – **he trusted himself to be real – and he told the truth.**

Of course, John Lennon isn't the only one who has dared to be so real, there are many other people who have been a great example to us in this way, and most of these have left great quotations we can continue to draw on for inspiration. I list loads of them on my

Goodreads (Jay Woodman) page, and also share some on my Radiance-Solutions website, and on my social media pages.

Art of any form – music, writing, painting, are the most obvious ones, but there are many more, (and we don't have to be 'artistic' to express ourselves, you could just write letters you may never post, or notes to yourself) – any of this helps us to truly face the world and explore it and the human psyche. We may begin with ambivalence, but we soon become fearless if we explore thoroughly enough. We become powerful in ourselves because we are learning to understand ourselves. We can't ever really hope to understand everything around us, but we can learn to understand ourselves in relation to anything else. If we know what we stand for and how we feel about things – then that never changes no matter what else changes around you – you become like a rock, yet at the same time feel floatingly free. (Of course if you do learn from new information and experiences or learn to respond differently to situations, your outlook does evolve, but you are still the floating rock that is you, growing as part of the conscious universe.)

You know we need variety in life to make it interesting. There has to be variety to even enable us to exist as individuals. So you stop blocking it off – you accept your curiosity and begin to explore, and the more you do this, the more you tend to then celebrate and appreciate the variety. You also accept your vulnerability, yet at the same time feel incredibly strong because you have opened fully to life. **Life feels magical – even in its madness and confusion – it is staggeringly intoxicating.**

So let's grasp the bull by the horns and dare to be real – you'll be amazed how great it will feel…. Not to be sucked in any more, not to be afraid any more. You will feel powerful, filled with energy, draw yourselves up, and take control of who you want to be.

Neale Donald Walsch said "You are all in the process of defining yourselves. Every act is an act of self definition."

Ralph Waldo Emerson said "To be yourself in a world that is constantly trying to make you something else is the greatest accomplishment."

And Shakespeare said "To thine own self be true, and it must follow, as the night the day, thou canst not then be false to any man."

John Lennon also said "There are two basic motivating forces: fear and love. When we are afraid, we pull back from life. When we are in love, we open to all that life has to offer with passion, excitement, and acceptance. We need to learn to love ourselves first, in all our glory and our imperfections. If we cannot love ourselves, we cannot fully open to our ability to love others or our potential to create. Evolution and all hopes for a better world rest in the fearlessness and open-hearted vision of people who embrace life."

* *

But wait a minute, just as with Lennon (and many others) – those in power don't want us to be real do they? They want us to go on consuming their goods (with poisons in them), and watching TV (with all the pap they'd like us to believe). They want us to feel powerless so that they can continue to lead us blindly into wars and other money making schemes, and so that we accept their laws and judgements, instead of questioning them or standing up for ourselves and our rights. **If we are real** then we become a threat to them, and they feel a need to deal with us – exactly, you got it – but now there are too many of us, and things are going to have to change. If we stop listening to them, if we stop using their systems, and simply walk away – that is all that is needed.

Then we will look after each other at community level – ensure we can access healthy food, work together at projects that sustain us – not them – keep things local – it makes much more sense. Trade our skills, make things that last, that don't waste raw materials and fuel, things that are truly useful – not junk to make profit out of others. We can take back everything they have been trying to take away from us bit by bit, over centuries, sneakily.

Marianne Williamson said "Do you really not know what to do? Or do you just lack the courage to do it?"

And Ghandi said "Be the change you wish to see in the world."

And Van Morrison said "You can't stop us on the road to freedom, you can't keep us 'cause our eyes can see."

And John Lennon said "You may say I'm a dreamer, but I'm not the only one. I hope some day you'll join us, and the world will live as one."

* *

Another thing Lennon taught us was never to be sucked into trying to fight those trying to exert power over us at their own game. He said "If you want peace, you won't get it with violence." And "There's no separation. We're all one. *Give peace a chance,* not *Shoot people for peace.* All you need is love. I believe it. It's damn hard, but I absolutely believe it."

So don't allow yourself to be diverted - firstly it infects you with their level of thinking, secondly it takes your power away. Save your power for doing the good stuff, dismiss the rest as insignificant. As long as you remain complete in who you want to be, you will keep your absolute power. The minute you slip into something else – you lose some of it to them. Don't give it away, keep you power quietly to yourself, and you will always be free, they cannot defeat you. No matter what they do, your power remains yours – they do not get a jot of it. Look at how we remember the great people like John Lennon – that's because they never lost anything at all. He has become untouchable, yet we can all grasp his dreams, and help make them as real as he believed they could be. He said "A dream you dream alone is only a dream, a dream you dream together is reality." And **"Peace is not something you wish for; It's something you make, something you do, something you are….."**

* *

More notes regarding depression.

Cognitive Dissonance[1] [1] might arise when you begin to realise there are things wrong in the world but can't see the whole picture so your bits don't fit or make sense, or you might be disappointed by the difference between your expectations and what has happened, or by people. As Lennon said **"The more real you get the more unreal the world gets."**

---

[1]

So you need to re-adjust. Surely allowing ourselves the time to do this rather than try to fight it is actually healthy? Look closely at how you are feeling and thinking. Express how you feel through safe means – artistically, or by speaking to a friend, therapist, or to an inanimate object or imaginary person, or by writing letters or notes. Even ask rhetorical questions, or ask for what you want to happen – it helps you clarify things and you might even find answers. Recognise your autonomy – you can seek clarification in your understanding, or you can actually just choose to change the way you want to feel or do things.

Medication obviously is useful in that it can give you the break to rest and steady yourself, before beginning to explore what is happening. If you view it as a tool to get back up a few steps, not as an excuse to just lie down at the bottom – then it is a positive and empowering act rather than something you are succumbing to. You should ideally always have a plan with your doctor to ensure that you are helped to withdraw carefully and gradually as you take back your power. You do sometimes need to be firm with your doctor about this, take responsibility for your own best interests, but never try to do it completely on your own.

Khalil Gibran wrote that "Your pain is the breaking of the shell that encloses your understanding."

Plug into the umbilical cord of power through meditation and recharge yourself. Connect with the beautiful energy of the planet too. **You are a rock between the earth and the reeling stars.** Stand there feeling it deeply. Reach out your arms, dance if you want to, swim in the moonlight, sing or shout. **Feel the processes in yourself re-adjusting, and renewing – and you will emerge with magic keys – re-enter life in the next stage of growing.**

Remember your connection with the harmonics of the universe. **You are one aspect of the one life force, manifested as human consciousness – everything else is a distraction.** Focus on your relationship with the life force and yourself – who you are being – how you want to be.

Other worries often pale into insignificance when you look at the bigger picture. You begin to realise that none of that small stuff can stop you from choosing exactly who you want to be. When you appreciate the astonishing variety of life around you, you tend to just find it easier to allow other things and people to just be as they are. **Reasoning doesn't matter so much anymore, even forgiving doesn't matter much anymore - because you see that there is no need, you just let go of the small stuff and walk on deep into the wonder of being fully alive.**

As John Lennon said: "Limitless undying love - which shines around me like a million suns - it calls me on and on across the universe."

FOOTNOTE:
1 - **Festinger's (1957)** cognitive dissonance theory suggests that we have an inner drive to hold all our attitudes and beliefs in harmony and avoid disharmony (or dissonance).

Cognitive dissonance refers to a situation involving conflicting attitudes, beliefs or behaviours. This produces a feeling of discomfort leading to an alteration in one of the attitudes, beliefs or behaviours to reduce the discomfort and restore balance etc.

"I wish I could show you when you are lonely,
or in the darkness, the astonishing light of your own being."
from a poem by Hafiz

YOU ARE THE ONE

*The new messenger is not some one special person to be born some day
whom we should pin our hopes upon – don't wait for the one to come for
the one is here already ...... in the many who are the one ....*

You are the messenger –
all you seek is within.
Each one of us has the power
and wisdom to live.

Inside us are all the answers,
the truth of who we are –
and all of our experiences
teach us more about ourselves.

We grow in each moment
more towards our centers
until like a candle flame
we are pure and absolute.

We flow with life, for we *are* life
and we love the world
for we *are* the world, and we *are* love
and we are everything and everyone.

Everything we do affects the whole
for our example and our belief
affects everyone we meet
as well as the collective consciousness

by which we are all connected
from our centers, to each other, and the universe –
and we are no more and no less than the next
for we are all one small part of the greatness.

And the flame grows as we feed it with life
for life begets new life and we evolve.
We need to move beyond
the destructive old limited foundations

of our political and economic systems,
our social and religious divisions,
and bring in new roots to grow with
so that they can become magnificent trees

with wonderful all inclusive, unlimited canopies
like the Tree of Life, embracing all people, beliefs and things,
swaying in the wind with understanding and giving,
instead of being stubbornly rigid, and breaking.

All ways lead to the same consciousness
which is the basis of Life and unconditional Love.
All should be free to live as they see fit,
not be terrified by dogma and false prophets.

All things vibrate with the energy of life –
let us learn to move together more harmoniously,
tuning in to the cosmic dance that sings
in our cells to entice us to listen more closely.

Let us look within our hearts and accept
our greatness as messengers, and yet be humble.
Let us spread the consciousness of evolution
to all systems before they crumble.

Everything is energy moving –
you are part of it all, spinning,
swirling, mixing; atoms of life
unlimited in its way of being.

The human race yearns to renew itself –
Will you dare to call in the highest vision
among your brethren, spread peace, joy, freedom?
Will you live your grandest truth, inspire, and awaken?

Yes, you are the messenger –
all you seek is within.
Each one of us has the power
and wisdom to truly live.

THE UNIVERSAL GAME

What would you say
if you were asked to play
this game called life?

Would you agree to be birthed,
to come down to earth
with all its woes and strife?

Could you really have known what it's like?
Would you have thought you could sort it all out,
or would have just done it for a laugh?

Would you have realised there was enough
beauty and goodness to balance it off,
make it an amazing experience?

If you could remember -
you must have thought it was some kind of adventure,
or at least a worthwhile choice to make -

or there's surely no way you'd have entered this game,
filled with extremities of love and pain,
and you probably wouldn't want to do it again.....

but, in the first sleep of death,
after rejoining our soul group, and a period
of review and reflection, I think we forget,

before we awake to a wider perspective

and set off to explore other directions and planes,
learning, and reporting back, between periods of resting....

so, when the time comes around
to journey back down,
we are ready to try once again.......

but I wonder, will we ever remember
that it's a study and growth opportunity,
so that we don't overreact to the immersion?

We are scouts of consciousness itself,
examining the outer fringes of universal expansion
and at the same time expanding from within.

Each time the soul goes home
we realise we are never alone, there, here, or anywhere.
We expand and circulate creatively together,

along with a multitude of evolving species,
feeding back to, and validating, the widening consciousness,
preventing the universe from collapsing on itself.

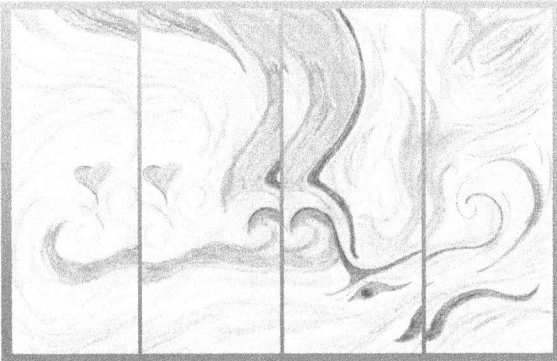

*"You can let go of all that stuff you thought was real when you know
it's just a game. What a relief, what a state of grace that brings."*
Joules

CONCLUSION

Awareness and Intention are probably the two most important things in developing consciousness. As you become increasingly aware, so your ability to create what you intend develops, because you develop an acute understanding of what does and doesn't work for you, as well as for others, and why. As you keep honing your awareness and learning from the experiences you create, you then also become more and more able to guide your own life in the way you wish.

We have also said that awareness of the world around you increases your capacity to enjoy and learn from everything. Being aware also means that we are bearing witness to the amazing imperative towards, and huge variety of, LIFE. You are in the stream of life itself and yet able to be an observer of it – the dreamer in the dream. But we are not just carried along by it; intention allows us to create the dream as we wish.

Basically, you could be aware without developing your powers of intention beyond a limited few choices, or you could have intent without being very aware, so not know how to achieve many of your intentions. For you to actually be able to develop consciously you have to do both in parallel, and then there are literally no limits.

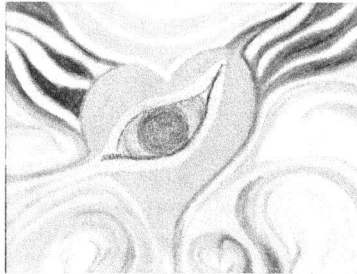

So, we can all be 'masters' of ourselves, through using awareness & intention to become more conscious, but we probably never arrive at the end of our journey, we continue to learn, just as the All of Everything that is and ever was continues to become more of itself. All of creation expands and evolves!

Personal development tools help us to learn to use our minds to help us rather than hinder us. We get to understand our emotional, mental, and physical selves more, and balance these with our heart-centred & spiritual selves. But we do not just sit in a retreat for too long – **we bring our balanced selves back into the world, and live in active engagement with it.**

That is what is happening today, not just on a personal level, but also at local community and global levels. People have evolved into international teams (regardless of any of the old senseless divisions) and are working together to help the whole of humanity, and the planet - to shift into a new phase of symbiosis so that we can all thrive.

Our 'Back to The Garden' open facebook group is just one of many good places to start to interact, and please do also join in on our other social media pages, such as Pinterest, Twitter, and many more. You can find links to many of these on the home page of our total wellbeing website www.radiance-solutions.co.uk

Blessings, Peace, and Good Luck - Julia

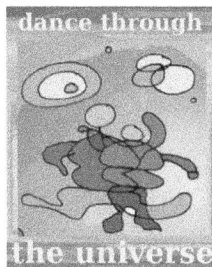

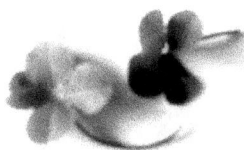

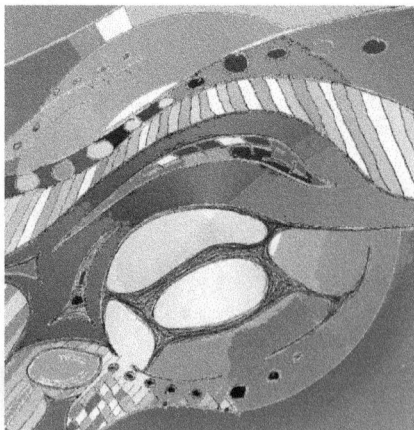

Before we go, here is a little info about other projects:

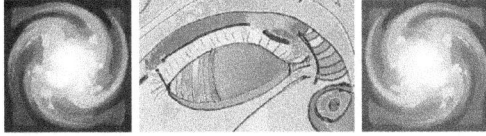

Already on Amazon (200 pages) - **My book "NO PARADOX – Living both In & Outside of The Matrix", discusses States of Consciousness and levels of Awareness, but it also puts forward the idea that we might be living in a construct (net, web, matrix) of paradoxes – with the stream of consciousness having spread out into apparent opposites.** This enables us (and thereby consciousness itself) to experience what life is like in its many different forms, and huge diversity of experiences.

Whether it is true or not, it is a hugely helpful idea, which enables us to step back a bit and view life in a more objective way instead of allowing ourselves to be tossed around by our subjective reactions to it. We are thus empowered to make much more conscious choices about how we live.

Imagine a character in a computer game waking up to the fact that he's in a game. Do you think he would just continue to do what he was programmed to do, or would he start to think and act for himself? Perhaps he'd be clever enough to pull a few tricks on the warlords who've been sending him off on secret trading missions with rebels, and start to build a plan of his own away from all the gun-smoke.

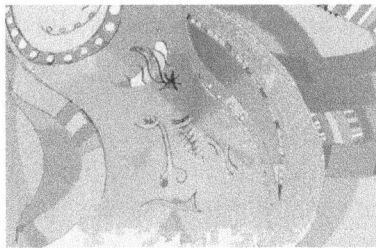

Coming next on Amazon **SACRED PERSPECTIVES** – another shortish manuscript I am preparing straight after this – full of goodies.

Apart from some novels I am working on, the next major work in progress is **"BACK TO THE GARDEN"** - already touched on. What if we could live consciously enough for our species to become truly viable – living in honest harmony with ourselves, each other, and the rest of the world around us? **"Back to The Garden"** will be looking at ways of doing this. In the meantime, our website - www.backtothegarden.org.uk - will be building up resources, information, and links to other helpful material and ideas along these lines. Our facebook group page "Back to The Garden" is an open group, welcoming input from members. Anyone can request to join in. We also schedule regular global meditation link-ups (subtle activism), to sow positive thought seeds into the collective consciousness.

I have had many poetry collections published over the years, some of which are still available directly from www.radiance-solutions.co.uk.

Also on my radiance-solutions website – are many more articles - some about depression, such as "Depression, Addiction, and even Weight issues, can be linked to Mineral Imbalance" (or "Hydration, Detoxification, and Cell Function") – and more about the **physical side of our Well-being**, such as "Holistic Wellbeing", plus ones about Communication, Stress, Relationships, and Loving & Respecting our Bodies.
Then there are also some about the **more Spiritual side**, such as "Lighter than this – Free-er than this – Getting into the Zone", "Spiritual Coaching", "Breathing to Balance Earth Grounding and Universal Source", "How we can feel Peaceful and Empowered enough to deal with almost anything", "Affirmations", and "The One arises through the Many, and the Many arise through the One".
There's also plenty of fun, creativity, poetry, and artwork,
plus various general Life Coaching advice, articles & tools.

www.ingramcontent.com/pod-product-compliance
Lightning Source LLC
Chambersburg PA
CBHW071627040426
42452CB00009B/1520